# DK First

# SPANISH

## Picture Dictionary

# Contents

LONDON, NEW YORK, MUNICH,
MELBOURNE, and DELHI

**Editor** Elise See Tai
**Project Editor** Anna Harrison
**Project Art Editors**
Ann Cannings, Emy Manby
**DTP Designer** David McDonald
**Production** Harriet Maxwell
**Translator** Roberto Rama with
Dylan Simanowitz

**Managing Editor**
Scarlett O'Hara

First published in Great Britain in 2005 by
Dorling Kindersley Limited
80 Strand, London WC2R 0RL

A Penguin Company

24681097531

Copyright ©2005 Dorling Kindersley Limited

ISBN 1-4053-1122-3

Colour reproduction by Colourscan, Singapore
Printed and bound in China by SNP Leefung

Discover more at
**www.dk.com**

# How to use this dictionary

Find out how you can get the most from your dictionary. At the beginning of the book there are Topic pages. These include lots of useful words on a particular subject, such as *Pets* and *In the Park*. Each word has its translation and help on how to pronounce it. The words on the Topic pages can be found in the English A–Z and in the Spanish A–Z. There are lots of other useful words here too. The verbs are in another section. At the back of the book there is a list of useful phrases for you to use when you practise your Spanish with your friends.

## Topic pages

topic heading

Spanish entry word

Spanish pronunciation

English translation

extra words on this subject

interesting fact

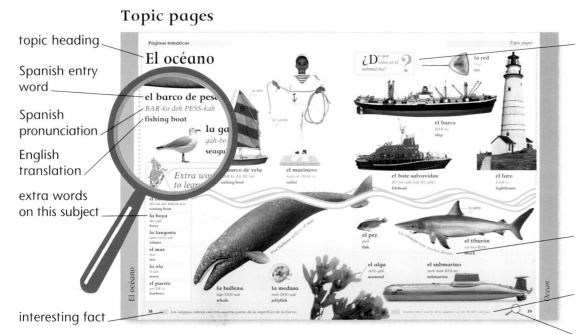

question for language practice

simple sentence with topic vocabulary

translation of interesting fact

*Look for me on the Topic pages!*

## English to Spanish A–Z

first word on the page with the Spanish translation

English entry word

Spanish translation

Spanish pronunciation

last word on the page with the Spanish translation

this shows the first letter of the words on the page

# Todo sobre mí

## All about me

*Soy alta.*

### el hermano
*air-MAH-no*
**brother**

**el bebé**
*beh-BEH*
**baby**

el abuelo
grandfather

la abuela
grandmother

### la hermana
*air-MAH-nah*
**sister**

### el padre
*PAH-dreh*
**father**

### la madre
*MAH-dreh*
**mother**

*Ésta es mi familia.*

**la niña**
*NEE-n'yah*
**child**

### los abuelos
*ah-boo'EH-los*
**grandparents**

*¡Somos felices!*

*Miguel está enfadado.*

### la tía
*TEE-ah*
**aunt**

### el tío
*TEE-o*
**uncle**

### feliz
*feh-LEETH*
**happy**

### enfadado
*en-fah-DAH-do*
**angry**

Hay alrededor de 206 huesos en el cuerpo humano.

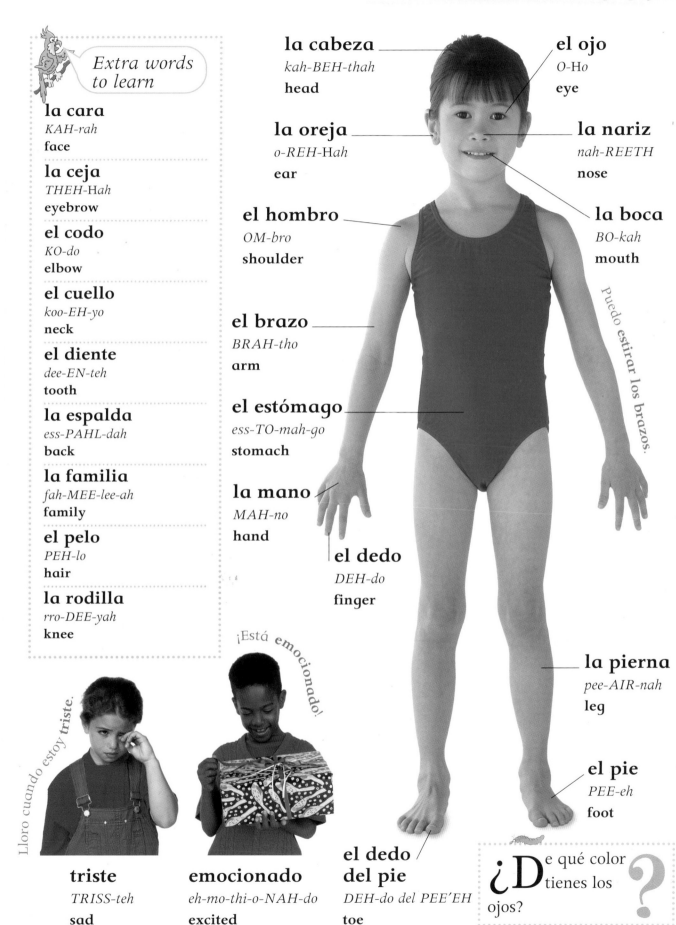

## Extra words to learn

**la cara**
*KAH-rah*
face

**la ceja**
*THEH-Hah*
eyebrow

**el codo**
*KO-do*
elbow

**el cuello**
*koo-EH-yo*
neck

**el diente**
*dee-EN-teh*
tooth

**la espalda**
*ess-PAHL-dah*
back

**la familia**
*fah-MEE-lee-ah*
family

**el pelo**
*PEH-lo*
hair

**la rodilla**
*rro-DEE-yah*
knee

**la cabeza**
*kah-BEH-thah*
head

**la oreja**
*o-REH-Hah*
ear

**el hombro**
*OM-bro*
shoulder

**el brazo**
*BRAH-tho*
arm

**el estómago**
*ess-TO-mah-go*
stomach

**la mano**
*MAH-no*
hand

**el dedo**
*DEH-do*
finger

**el ojo**
*O-Ho*
eye

**la nariz**
*nah-REETH*
nose

**la boca**
*BO-kah*
mouth

*Puedo estirar los brazos.*

**la pierna**
*pee-AIR-nah*
leg

**el pie**
*PEE-eh*
foot

*Lloro cuando estoy triste.*

**triste**
*TRISS-teh*
sad

*¡Está emocionado!*

**emocionado**
*eh-mo-thi-o-NAH-do*
excited

**el dedo del pie**
*DEH-do del PEE'EH*
toe

¿**D**e qué color tienes los ojos?

*There are about 206 bones in the body.*

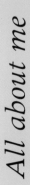

*All about me*

5

# La ropa
## Clothes

**los calcetínes**
*kal-theh-TEE-nes*
socks

**la blusa**
*BLOO-sah*
blouse

**la bota**
*BO-tah*
boot

**las gafas**
*GAH-fahs*
glasses

**el jersey**
*Her-SAY*
jumper

**el pijama**
*pee-HAH-mah*
pyjamas

**la ropa interior**
*RRO-pah in-TEH-ree-OR*
underwear

**el vestido**
*bess-TEE-do*
dress

**el zapato**
*thah-PAH-to*
shoe

el botón
button

**la camisa**
*kah-MEE-sah*
shirt

la cremallera
zip

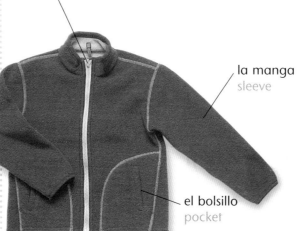

la manga
sleeve

el bolsillo
pocket

**el forro polar**
*FOR-rro po-LAR*
fleece

**los vaqueros**
*bah-KEH-ross*
jeans

El abrigo me abriga.

**la bufanda**
*boo-FAN-dah*
scarf

el guante
glove

**el abrigo**
*ah-BREE-go*
coat

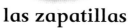

**las zapatillas**
*thah-pah-TEE-yahs*
trainers

La ropa

Los vaqueros tienen más de 130 años!

el cinturón
belt

**los pantalones
cortos**

*pan-tah-LO-nes KOR-tos*

**shorts**

**el bañador**

*bah-n'yah-DOR*

**swimsuit**

**la camiseta**

*kah-mee-SEH-tah*

**T-shirt**

**los pantalones**

*pahn-tah-LO-ness*

**trousers**

**la chaqueta**

*chah-KEH-tah*

**jacket**

la capucha
hood

**la falda**

*FAHL-dah*

**skirt**

**el impermeable**

*im-pair-meh-AH-bleh*

**raincoat**

los vaqueros
jeans

Los vaqueros y las zapatillas son mi ropa favorita.

**las catiuscas**

*kah-tee-OOS-kahs*

**wellington boots**

¿**Q**ué te gusta llevar zapatos o zapatillas?

*Jeans are more than 130 years old!*

*Clothes*

# La cocina

## Kitchen

**la sartén**
*sar-TEN*
**frying pan**

**el plato**
*PLAH-to*
**plate**

el horno
oven

la olla
saucepan

**la cocina**
*ko-THI-nah*
**cooker**

**la cuchara**
*koo-CHAH-rah*
**spoon**

**la taza**
*TAH-thah*
**mug**

el libro
book

**el paño de cocina**
*PAH-n'yo de ko-THI-nah*
**tea towel**

**el cuenco**
*koo'EN-ko*
**bowl**

**la olla**
*O-yah*
**saucepan**

¿Qué hay en la cuchara?

La primera cocina de gas se hizo en 1826.

*Gracias* por fregar *los platos*.

el armario
cupboard

## el fregadero

*freh-gah-DEH-ro*

**sink**

el congelador
freezer

### Extra words to learn

**la bandeja**
*bahn-DEH-Hah*
**tray**

**el cubo de la basura**
*KOO-bo deh lah BAH-soo-rah*
**bin**

**el hervidor de agua**
*air-be-DOR deh AH-goo'ah*
**kettle**

**la jarra**
*HAH-rrah*
**jug**

**la lavadora**
*lah-bah-DOR-ah*
**washing machine**

**la plancha**
*PLAHN-chah*
**iron**

**la taza**
*TAH-thah*
**cup**

**el tostador**
*toss-tah-DOR*
**toaster**

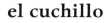

## el cuchillo

*koo-CHEE-yo*

**knife**

## el tenedor

*teh-neh-DOR*

**fork**

## el frigorífico

*free-go-REE-fee-ko*

**fridge**

¿Te gusta hacer **pasteles** al horno?

### el mandil

*mahn-DEEL*

**apron**

### el guante del horno

*goo'AHN-teh dell OR-no*

**oven glove**

### el vaso

*BAH-so*

**glass**

# El cuarto de baño

## Bathroom

**el peine**
*PEH'eh-neh*
comb

**el baño**
*BAHN-n'yo*
bath

**el juguete**
*Hoo-GEH-teh*
toy

**el agua**
*AH-goo-ah*
water

Pongo **pasta de dientes** en el **cepillo de dientes**.

**la esponja**
*es-PON-Hah*
sponge

**las toallas**
*to'AH-yahs*
towels

el tubo
tube

**la pasta de dientes**
*PAHS-tah deh dee-EN-tess*
toothpaste

**el cepillo de dientes**
*theh-PEE-yo deh dee-EN-tess*
toothbrush

¿**C**uántas cosas amarillas hay en esta página?

10

¡El cuarto de baño más caro tiene un inodoro de oro!

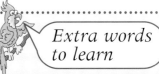

**Extra words to learn**

**el cepillo del pelo**
*theh-PEE-yo del PEH-lo*
**hairbrush**

**la colada**
*ko-LAH-dah*
**washing**

**el maquillaje**
*mah-kee-YAH-Heh*
**make-up**

**los pañuelos de papel**
*pah-n'yoo-EH-loss deh pah-PEL*
**tissues**

**el tapón**
*tah-PON*
**plug**

**la toallita**
*to-ah-YEE-tah*
**flannel**

**el champú**
*cham-POO*
**shampoo**

**el espejo**
*ess-PEH-Ho*
**mirror**

**la ducha**
*DOO-chah*
**shower**

**el papel higiénico**
*pah-PEL ee-He-EN-ee-ko*
**toilet paper**

**el jabón**
*Hah-BON*
**soap**

**el inodoro**
*ee-no-DOO-ro*
**toilet**

**el grifo**
*GREE-fo*
**tap**

la toallita
flannel

el jabón
soap

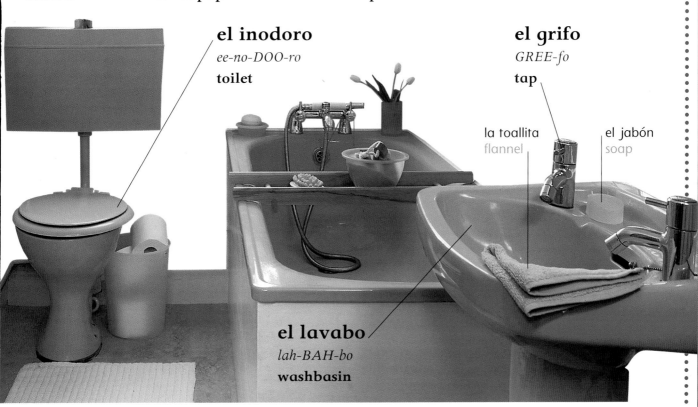

**el lavabo**
*lah-BAH-bo*
**washbasin**

*The most expensive bathroom has a gold toilet!*

**Bathroom**

11

## el despertador
*dess-pair-tah-DOOR*
**alarm clock**

## la cama
*KAH-mah*
**bed**

## la almohada
*ahl-mo-AH-dah*
**pillow**

## el edredón
*eh-dreh-DON*
**duvet**

## la silla
*SEE-yah*
**chair**

# Mi habitación
*My bedroom*

## la cómoda
*KO-mo-dah*
**chest of drawers**

Duermo en la cama.

## el videojuego
*be-deh-o-Hoo'EH-go*
**computer game**

Hacemos juegos de mesa.

el ajedrez
chess

¿Qué hay en el armario?

la alfombra
*ahl-FOM-brah*
rug

La moqueta es azul.

los libros
*LEE-bros*
books

Puedo tocar la guitarra.

el armario
*ar-MAH-ree-o*
wardrobe

la guitarra
*ghee-TAH-rah*
guitar

la percha
*PER-chah*
coat hanger

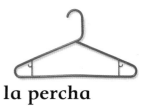

la lámpara
*LAHM-pah-rah*
lamp

el espejo
*ess-PEH-Ho*
mirror

# El jardín
## *Garden*

**la carretilla**
*kar-rreh-TEE-yah*
**wheelbarrow**

**el árbol**
*AR-bol*
**tree**

el tronco
trunk

**el rastrillo**
*rrahs-TREE-yo*
**rake**

el banco
bench

**el césped**
*THESS-ped*
**grass**

**el cortacésped**
*kor-tah-THESS-ped*
**lawn mower**

*Extra words to learn*

**el bulbo**
*BOOL-bo*
**bulb**

**el césped**
*THESS-ped*
**lawn**

**el invernadero**
*in-bair-nah-DEH-ro*
**greenhouse**

**la jardinera**
*Har-dee-NEH-rah*
**gardener**

**la maceta**
*mah-THEH-tah*
**flowerpot**

**la paleta**
*pah-LEH-tah*
**trowel**

**la regadera**
*reh-gah-DEH-rah*
**watering can**

**la valla**
*BAH-yah*
**fence**

Normalmente las mariposas vuelan de día y las polillas de noche.

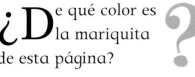

¿**D**e qué color es la mariquita de esta página?

la concha
*shell*

**el caracol**
*kah-rah-KOL*
**snail**

**la lombriz**
*lom-BREETH*
**worm**

el ala
*wing*

**la mariposa**
*mah-ree-PO-sah*
**butterfly**

**la abeja**
*ah-BEH-Hah*
**bee**

**la semilla**
*seh-MEE-yah*
**seed**

**la mariquita**
*mah-ree-KEE-tah*
**ladybird**

*Las flores* están saliendo en **el jardín**.

*Lucia está* **excavando** *en el jardín.*

**la flor**
*flor*
**flower**

**la oruga**
*o-ROO-gah*
**caterpillar**

**la tierra**
*tee-EH-rrah*
**soil**

**la pala**
*PAH-lah*
**spade**

*Usually butterflies fly in the day and moths fly at night.*

*Garden*

# La vida en la ciudad
*City life*

**la casa**
*KAH-sah*
house

**el autobús**
*ah'oo-to-BOOS*
coach

¿**Q**ué hora tiene el reloj azul?

**el rascacielos**
*rahs-kah-thi-EH-los*
skyscaper

*Las ciudades tienen edificios altos que se llaman rascacielos.*

**el bloque de pisos**
*BLOH-keh deh PEE-sos*
flats

**el reloj**
*rreh-LOH*
clock

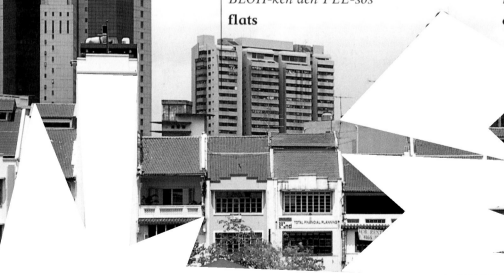

**la calle**
*KAH-yeh*
street

**la tienda**
*tee-EN-dah*
shop

Tokio, en Japón, es la ciudad más grande del mundo.

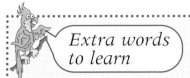

**Extra words to learn**

**la acera**
*ah-THEH-rah*
**pavement**

**la autopista**
*ah'oo-to-PISS-tah*
**motorway**

**el banco**
*BAHN-ko*
**bank**

**la cafetería**
*kah-feh-teh-REE-ah*
**café**

**el coche**
*KO-cheh*
**car**

**la fábrica**
*FAH-bree-kah*
**factory**

**el metro**
*MEH-tro*
**underground railway**

**la parada de autobús**
*pah-RAH-dah deh ah'oo-to-BOOS*
**bus stop**

**el teléfono**
*teh-LEH-fo-no*
**phone**

**la señal**
*seh-N'YAHL*
**sign**

**el semáforo**
*seh-MAH-for-rro*
**traffic lights**

**la farola**
*fah-RO-lah*
**street light**

**el cine**
*THI-neh*
**cinema**

**el cruce**
*KROO-theh*
**crossing**

**el taxi**
*TAK-see*
**taxi**

**el hotel**
*o-TELL*
**hotel**

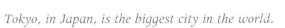

*Tokyo, in Japan, is the biggest city in the world.*

**la cometa**
*ko-MEH-tah*
kite

**la cuerda**
*koo'AIR-dah*
skipping rope

**el monopatín**
*mo-no-pah-TEEN*
skateboard

**las flores**
*FLO-res*
flowers

**el carrusel**
*kar-rroo-SEL*
roundabout

# En el parque
## *In the park*

¡Me encanta saltar a **la cuerda**!

¿Tienes una **cometa**?

**la niña**
*NEE-n'yah*
girl

Tres **niños** están **jugando** en **el carrusel**.

**actuar**
*ack-too-AR*
**acting**

**cantar**
*kan-TAR*
**singing**

**el ciclismo**
*thee-KLEES-mo*
**cycling**

**la cocina**
*ko-THI-nah*
**cooking**

**el coleccionismo**
*ko-lek-thi-o-NISS-mo*
**collecting**

**el dibujo**
*dee-BOO-Ho*
**drawing**

**la lectura**
*lek-TOO-rah*
**reading**

**viajar**
*be-ah-HAR*
**travelling**

**la escritura**
*ess-kree-TOO-rah*
**writing**

¿**C**uál es tu hobby favorito?

*En gimnasia salto y me estiro.*

**el surf**
*soorf*
**surfing**

**la gimnasia**
*Hem-NAH-see-ah*
**gymnastics**

**sacar una foto**
*sah-KAR oona FO-to*
**taking a photo**

**pintar**
*pin-TAR*
**painting**

# La comida

## *Food*

la piel
skin

### el plátano
*PLAH-tah-no*
banana

### la naranja
*nah-RAHN-Hah*
orange

### la manzana
*mahn-THAH-nah*
apple

### la sandía
*sahn-DEE-ah*
watermelon

### el tomate
*to-MAH-teh*
tomato

### la zanahoria
*than-nah-O-ree-yah*
carrot

### la lechuga
*leh-CHOO-gah*
lettuce

### el repollo
*rreh-PO-yo*
cabbage

*Estamos comiendo spaghetti.*

el plato
plate

el cuenco
bowl

el vaso
glass

el cuchillo
knife

el tenedor
fork

la silla
chair

la mesa
table

*La piña es una fruta.*

### la piña
*PEE-n'yah*
pineapple

La zanahoria es una verdura y una raíz.

**la patata**
*pah-TAH-tah*
potato

**el huevo**
*oo'EH-bo*
egg

**el yogur**
*yo-GOOR*
yoghurt

**la leche**
*LEH-cheh*
milk

**la mermelada**
*mair-meh-LAH-dah*
jam

¿**Q**ué tomas para desayunar? **?**

*Me gusta el pan con miel.*

**el pan**
*pahn*
bread

**la mantequilla**
*mahn-teh-KEE-yah*
butter

**la miel**
*mee-ELL*
honey

*Extra words to learn*

**el azúcar**
*ah-THOO-kar*
sugar

**la cebolla**
*theh-BO-yah*
onion

**la ensalada**
*en-sah-LAH-dah*
salad

**la fruta**
*FROO-tah*
fruit

**la galleta**
*gah-YEH-tah*
biscuit

**la harina**
*ah-REE-nah*
flour

**el pollo**
*PO-yo*
chicken

**el spaghetti**
*ess-pah-GEH-tee*
spaghetti

**la verdura**
*bair-DOO-rah*
vegetable

**la pasta**
*PAHS-tah*
pasta

el arroz
rice

**la carne**
*KAR-neh*
meat

*A carrot is a vegetable and a root.*

*Food*

# De compras
## *Shopping*

**el mercado**
*mair-KAH-do*
market

el precio
price

**el dinero**
*dee-NEH-ro*
money

**la bolsa de la compra**
*BOHL-sah deh la KOM-prah*
shopping bag

Tengo que **comprar** algo de comida.

Estamos **esperando** en la cola.

**el carrito**
*kar-RREE-to*
trolley

**la cesta**
*THESS-tah*
basket

**24**  El primer carrito de la compra se inventó hace más de 60 años.

## la camarera
*kah-mah-REH-rah*
**waitress**

## la cafetería
*kah-feh-tah-REE-ah*
**café**

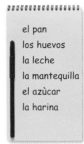

el pan
los huevos
la leche
la mantequilla
el azùcar
la harina

## la lista de la compra
*LISS-tah deh la KOM-prah*
**shopping list**

## el supermercado
*soo-pair-mair-KAH-do*
**supermarket**

## la panadería
*pah-nah-deh-REE-ah*
**bakery**

## la librería
*lee-breh-REE-ah*
**bookshop**

*Tiene muchas bolsas.*

## la compradora
*kom-prah-DOR-ah*
**shopper**

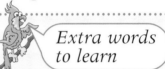

*Extra words to learn*

## la caja
*KAH-Hah*
**till**

## la cuenta
*koo'EN-tah*
**bill**

## el dependiente
*deh-pen-dee-EN-teh*
**shop assistant**

## el dinero (en efectivo)
*dee-NEH-ro en eh-fek-TEE-bo*
**cash**

## ir de compras
*eer deh KOM-prahs*
**to go shopping**

## el precio
*PREH-thi-o*
**price**

## el recibo
*rreh-THI-bo*
**receipt**

## la tienda
*tee-EN-dah*
**shop**

*The first shopping trolley was invented more than 60 years ago.*

## la bebida

*beh-BEE-dah*

**drink**

## los sándwiches

*SAND-wee-ches*

**sandwiches**

## las tarjetas de cumpleaños

*tar-HEH-tahs deh koom-pleh-AH-n'yos*

**birthday cards**

## las velas

*BEH-lahs*

**candles**

## la tarta de cumpleaños

*TAR-tah deh koom-pleh-AH-n'yos*

**birthday cake**

# En la fiesta

## *At the party*

Es divertido **jugar** con **globos**.

Nos gusta **bailar** con **la música**.

### el reproductor de CD

*rreh-pro-dook-TOR deh theh-DEH*

**CD player**

### el mago

*MAH-go*

**magician**

## los adornos
*ah-DOR-nos*
**decorations**

¡Feliz Cumpleaños!

¡Eso es increíble!

Quiero abrir **los regalos**.

## los regalos
*rreh-GAH-los*
**presents**

## los globos
*GLO-bos*
**balloons**

## la cámara
*KAH-mah-rah*
**camera**

## las galletas
*gah-YEH-tahs*
**biscuits**

## el helado
*eh-LAH-do*
**ice cream**

## los dulces
*DOOL-thehs*
**sweets**

# El tiempo libre

## *Free time*

### juego de mesa
*Hoo'AY-go deh MEH-sah*
**board game**

### el balón
*bah-LON*
**ball**

### el robot
*rro-BOT*
**robot**

**el escondite**
*ess-kon-DEE-teh*
**hide-and-seek**

**el juego**
*Hoo'EH-go*
**game**

**el juguete**
*Hoo-GEH-teh*
**toy**

**el libro**
*LEE-bro*
**book**

**la marioneta**
*mah-ree-o-NEH-tah*
**puppet**

**la máscara**
*MAHS-kah-rah*
**mask**

**la muñeca**
*moo-N'YEH-kah*
**doll**

**el patinaje**
*pah-tee-NAH-Heh*
**skating**

### los dados
*DAH-dos*
**dice**

### el (ordenador) portátil
*(or-den-a-DOR)*
*por-TAH-til*
**laptop**

*Juego con el tren.*

el tren
train

el lápiz de color
coloured pencil

### el dibujo
*dee-BOO-Ho*
**drawing**

### el rompecabezas
*rrom-peh-kah-BEH-thas*
**puzzle**

### el tren de juguete
*tren deh Hoo-GEH-teh*
**train set**

El primer ordenador portátil se hizo hace más de 20 años.

### las cartas
*KAR-tahs*
**cards**

### los CDs
*theh-DEHS*
**CDs**

### el reproductor de cd
*rreh-pro-dook-TOR
deh theh-DEH*
**CD player**

### los videojuegos
*be-deh-o-Hoo'EH-gos*
**computer games**

el casco
helmet

¡Se mueve muy rápido!

### el patinaje en línea
*pah-tee-NAH-Heh en
LEE-nee-ah*
**rollerblading**

la marioneta
puppet

### el teatro de marionetas
*tee-AH-tro deh
mah-ree-o-NEH-tah*
**puppet show**

### el disfraz
*diss-FRATH*
**fancy dress**

el osito de
peluche
teddy bear

¿Te gustan los videojuegos?

*The first laptop was made more than 20 years ago.*

*Free time*

# El transporte
## Transport

**el avión**
*ah-be-ON*
plane

**el ferry**
*FEH-rree*
ferry

**el barco de vela**
*BAR-ko deh BE-lah*
sailing boat

**el taxi**
*TAK-see*
taxi

**el camión**
*kah-mee-ON*
lorry

**la bici**
*BE-thi*
bike

*Un autobús lleva a la gente de viaje.*

**el autobús**
*ah'oo-to-BOOS*
bus

# Al rescate
## To the rescue

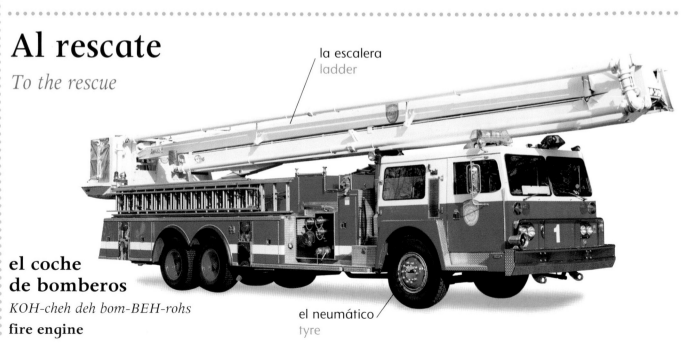

la escalera
ladder

**el coche
de bomberos**
*KOH-cheh deh bom-BEH-rohs*
fire engine

el neumático
tyre

¡El coche de bomberos más rápido alcanzó los 655 km por hora en 1998!

Un globo aerostático flota en el cielo.

## el globo aerostático
*GLOH-bo ah'eh-ro-STAH-tee-ko*
**hot-air balloon**

## el tren
*tren*
**train**

**el billete**
*be-YEH-teh*
**ticket**

**el bote**
*BO-teh*
**boat**

**la camioneta**
*kah-mee-o-NEH-tah*
**van**

**el cohete espacial**
*ko-EH-teh ess-pah-thi-AHL*
**space rocket**

**el combustible**
*kom-booss-TEE-bleh*
**fuel**

**el garaje**
*gah-RAH-Heh*
**garage**

**el horario**
*o-RAH-ree-o*
**timetable**

**el viaje**
*be-AH-Heh*
**journey**

el equipaje
luggage

el espejo
mirror

## el coche
*KO-cheh*
**car**

## la motocicleta
*mo-to-thi-KLEH-tah*
**motorbike**

¿**C**uántas ruedas hay en esta página?

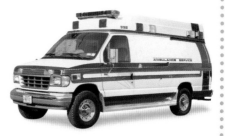

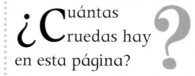

## el helicóptero de la policía
*eh-lee-KOP-teh-ro deh lah po-lee-THI-ah*
**police helicopter**

## el coche de la policía
*KO-cheh deh lah po-lee-THI-ah*
**police car**

## la ambulancia
*ahm-boo-LAN-thi-ah*
**ambulance**

*The fastest fire engine reached 655 kilometres per hour in 1998!*

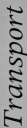

*Transport*

# Animales de la selva

*Jungle animals*

**el colibrí**
*ko-lee-BREE*
**hummingbird**

el ala
wing

**el chimpancé**
*chim-pahn-THEH*
**chimpanzee**

**el murciélago**
*moor-thi-EH-lah-go*
**bat**

**la mariposa**
*mah-ree-PO-sah*
**butterfly**

**la hormiga**
*or-MEE-gah*
**ant**

**la araña**
*ah-RAH-n'yah*
**spider**

**el gorila**
*goh-REE-lah*
**gorilla**

**la polilla**
*po-LEE-yah*
**moth**

¿**C**uántos
**C**animales
hay en esta página?

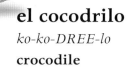

**el cocodrilo**
*ko-ko-DREE-lo*
**crocodile**

Animales de la selva

La selva más grande del mundo está en Suramérica.

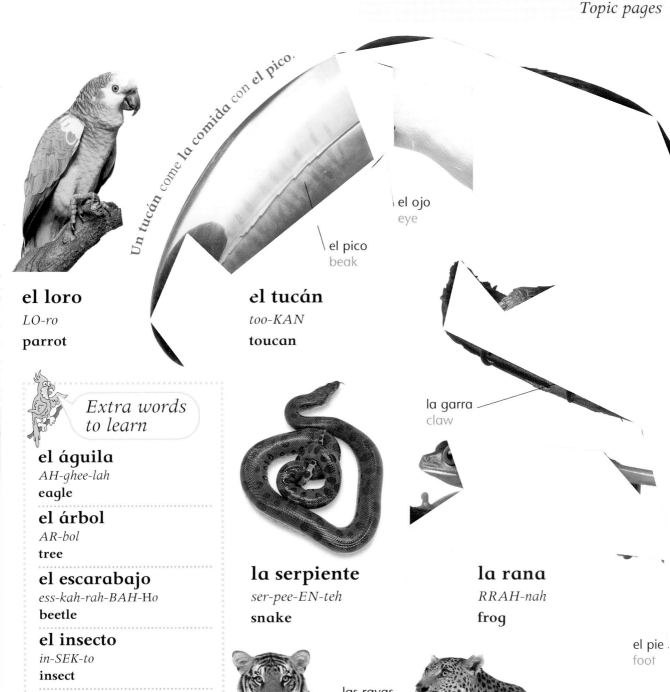

Un tucán come la comida con el pico.

el ojo
eye

el pico
beak

la garra
claw

el pie
foot

**el loro**
*LO-ro*
**parrot**

**el tucán**
*too-KAN*
**toucan**

la serpiente
*ser-pee-EN-teh*
**snake**

**la rana**
*RRAH-nah*
**frog**

las rayas
stripes

**el tigre**
*TEE-greh*
**tiger**

**el leopardo**
*leh-o-PAR-do*
**leopard**

## Extra words to learn

**el águila**
*AH-ghee-lah*
**eagle**

**el árbol**
*AR-bol*
**tree**

**el escarabajo**
*ess-kah-rah-BAH-Ho*
**beetle**

**el insecto**
*in-SEK-to*
**insect**

**la lagartija**
*lah-gar-TEE-Hah*
**lizard**

**el mamífero**
*mah-MEE-feh-ro*
**mammal**

**salvaje**
*sahl-BAH-Heh*
**wild**

**la selva tropical**
*SEL-bah tro-pee-KAHL*
**rainforest**

*Jungle animals*

*The biggest jungle in the world is in South America.*

# Animales del mundo

## *World animals*

Extra words to learn

**el koala**
*ko-AH-lah*
koala

**el ciervo**
*thi-AIR-bo*
deer

**el babuino**
*bah-boo-E'NO*
baboon

**el búho**
*BOO-o*
owl

**el caimán**
*kah'e-MAN*
alligator

**el halcón**
*ahl-KON*
hawk

la pata
paw

**el lobo**
*LO-bo*
wolf

**el pelícano**
*peh-LEE-kah-no*
pelican

**la rata**
*RAH-tah*
rat

**el zorro**
*THO-rro*
fox

**el panda**
*PAN-dah*
panda

**el león**
*leh-ON*
lion

¡Una jirafa tiene el cuello largo!

**la jirafa**
*He-RAH-fah*
giraffe

el pico
beak

la cola
tail

**el pingüino**
*pin-goo'E-no*
penguin

**el oso polar**
*O-so po-LAR*
polar bear

¿**C**uántos pájaros hay en esta página?

¡Una jirafa tiene el mismo número de huesos en el cuello que tú!

Animales del mundo

*Un elefante come la comida con **la trompa**.*

**el camello**
*kah-MEH-yo*
**camel**

las rayas
stripes

**la cebra**
*THEH-brah*
**zebra**

la trompa
trunk

**el elefante**
*eh-leh-FAN-teh*
**elephant**

**el canguro**
*kan-GOO-ro*
**kangaroo**

la cola
tail

**el oso**      la garra
*O-so*          claw
**bear**

**el delfín**
*del-FEEN*      la aleta
**dolphin**     flipper

**el rinoceronte**
*ree-no-theh-RON-teh*
**rhinoceros**

*A giraffe has the same number of bones in its neck as you!*

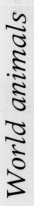

**el prado**
*PRAH-do*
field

**el tractor**
*trak-TOR*
tractor

**el trigo**
*TREE-go*
wheat

**los corderos**
*kor-DEH-rohs*
lambs

**el perro pastor**
*PEH-rroh pahs-TOR*
sheepdog

# En la granja
## On the farm

La agricultora utiliza **el tractor**.

**la agricultora**
*ah-gree-kool-TOR-ah*
farmer

Cristina le da **leche** al **cordero**.

La vaca come hierba en el prado.

## la cosechadora
*ko-seh-chah-DOO-rah*
**combine harvester**

## la valla
*BAH-yah*
**fence**

El caballo es marrón y blanco.

Las vacas pequeñas se llaman **terneras**.

## el pato
*PAH-to*
**duck**

El pollito está cerca de su madre.

## la vaca
*BAH-kah*
**cow**

## la paja
*PAH-Hah*
**hay**

## el caballo
*kah-BAH-yo*
**horse**

## el pollo
*PO-yo*
**chicken**

## los patitos
*pah-TEE-tos*
**ducklings**

# El océano

*Ocean*

### el barco de pesca
*BAR-ko deh PESS-kah*
**fishing boat**

### la gaviota
*gah-be-O-tah*
**seagull**

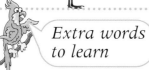

> **Extra words to learn**

**el ancla**
*AHN-klah*
anchor

**el bote de remos**
*BO-teh deh RREH-mos*
rowing boat

**la boya**
*BO-yah*
buoy

**la langosta**
*lahn-GOSS-tah*
lobster

**el mar**
*mar*
sea

**la ola**
*O-lah*
wave

**el puerto**
*poo'ER-to*
harbour

La vela es amarilla y púrpura.

la vela
sail

### el barco de vela
*BAR-ko deh BE-lah*
**sailing boat**

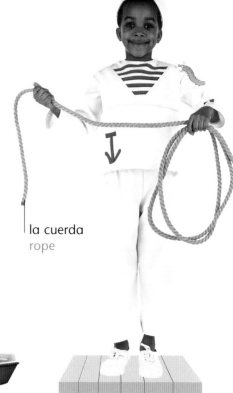

la cuerda
rope

### el marinero
*mah-ree-NEH-ro*
**sailor**

Una ballena nada en el mar.

### la ballena
*bah-YEH-nah*
**whale**

### la medusa
*meh-DOO-sah*
**jellyfish**

El océano

Los océanos cubren casi tres cuartas partes de la superficie de la tierra.

¿**D**e qué color es el submarino? **?**

**la red**
*rred*
net

**el barco**
*BAR-ko*
ship

**el bote salvavidas**
*BO-teh sahl-bah-BE-dahs*
lifeboat

**el faro**
*FAH-ro*
lighthouse

la aleta
fin

**el pez**
*peth*
fish

*Un tiburón tiene muchos dientes.*

**el tiburón**
*tee-boo-RON*
shark

**el alga**
*AHL-gah*
seaweed

**el submarino**
*soob-mah-REE-no*
submarine

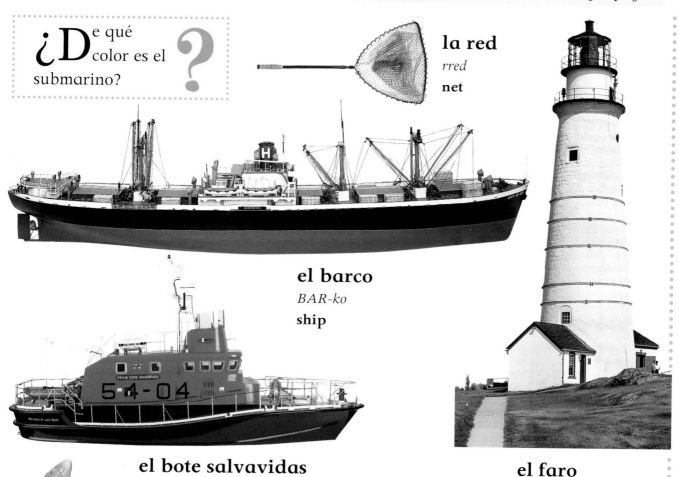
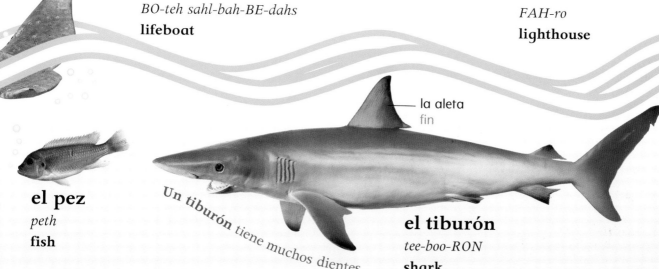
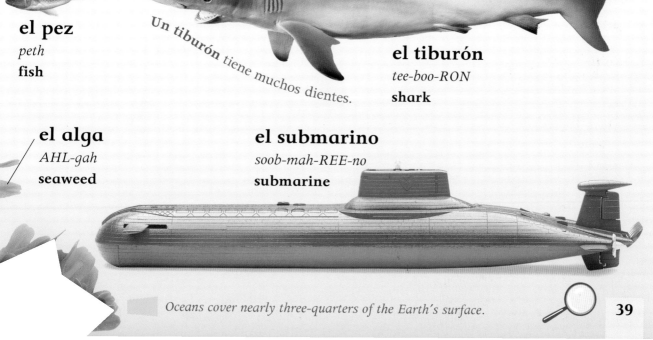

*Oceans cover nearly three-quarters of the Earth's surface.*

*Ocean*

# La naturaleza

## *Nature*

Un nenúfar crece en el agua.

el pico
beak

**el pato**
*PAH-to*
**duck**

**la planta**
*PLAHN-tah*
**plant**

**la libélula**
*lee-BEH-loo-lah*
**dragonfly**

**el nenúfar**
*neh-NOO-far*
**water lily**

Muchos **animales** viven cerca de **estanques**.

**el cisne**
*THISS-neh*
**swan**

**el sapo**
*SAH-po*
**toad**

Los sapos generalmente tienen la piel áspera y

*Los renacuajos nadan en estanques.*

la antena
antenna

¿**C**uántos
**C**nenúfares
hay en el estanque? **?**

el ala
wing

**el nido**
*NEE-do*
**nest**

**los renacuajos**
*rreh-nah-koo′AH-Hos*
**tadpoles**

**la avispa**
*ah-BISS-pah*
**wasp**

**la mosca**
*MOSS-kah*
**fly**

*Extra words
to learn*

**el estanque**
*ess-TAN-keh*
**pond**

**el búho**
*BOO-o*
**owl**

**la rana**
*RRAH-nah*
**frog**

**el agua**
*AH-goo-ah*
**water**

**el conejo**
*ko-NEH-Ho*
**rabbit**

**la garza real**
*GAR-thah rreh-AHL*
**heron**

**el hábitat**
*AH-be-tat*
**habitat**

**el insecto**
*in-SEK-to*
**insect**

**la mala hierba**
*MAH-lah ee-AIR-bah*
**weed**

**la mariposa**
*mah-ree-PO-sah*
**butterfly**

**el pájaro**
*PAH-Hah-ro*
**bird**

*Toads usually have rough skin and frogs have smooth skin.*

*Nature*

**el cubo**
*KOO-boh*
bucket

**la pala**
*PAH-lah*
spade

**el cangrejo**
*kahn-GREH-Ho*
crab

**la concha**
*KON-chah*
shell

**las piedras**
*pee-EH-drahs*
pebbles

# En la playa
## *At the beach*

Me encanta **nadar** en **el mar**.

¿Te gusta ir a **la playa**?

**la roca**
*RRO-kah*
rock

la crema solar
suncream

**las gaviotas**
*gah-be-O-tahs*
seagulls

Nos encanta **jugar** con la arena.

Llevo **gafas de nadar**.

el bañador
trunks

**la estrella de mar**
*ess-TREH-yah deh mar*
starfish

**el helado**
*eh-LAH-do*
ice cream

**el alga**
*AHL-gah*
seaweed

Estamos haciendo **un castillo de arena**.

**las gafas de nadar**
*GAH-fahs deh nah-DAR*
goggles

**la tumbona**
*toom-BO-nah*
deck chair

**la pamela**
*pah-MEH-lah*
sunhat

**la arena**
*ah-REH-nah*
sand

**el castillo de arena**
*kahs-TEE-yo deh ah-REH-nah*
sandcastle

# La escuela
## *School*

### las tijeras
*tee-HEH-rahs*
scissors

### los lápices de colores
*LAH-pee-thess deh ko-LOR-cs*
coloured pencils

### la pizarra
*pee-THAR-rrah*
blackboard

### la regla
*RREG-lah*
ruler

### la goma de borrar
*GO-mah deh bor-RRAR*
rubber

### el lápiz
*LAH-pith*
pencil

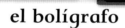

### el bolígrafo
*bo-LEE-grah-fo*
pen

la libreta
notebook

### el escritorio
*ess-kree-TO-ree-o*
desk

*Extra words to learn*

**el alfabeto**
*ahl-fah-BEH-to*
alphabet

**el aula**
*ah'OO-lah*
classroom

**la ciencia**
*thi-EN-thi-ah*
science

**el dibujo**
*dee-BOO-Ho*
drawing

**la escritura**
*ess-kree-TOO-rah*
writing

**la lectura**
*lek-TOO-rah*
reading

**la profesora**
*pro-feh-SOR-ah*
teacher

**la silla**
*SEE-yah*
chair

El lápiz más largo del mundo mide casi 20 metros.

¿*Puedes ver mi comida?*

## la fiambrera
*fee-am-BREH-rah*
**lunch box**

¿**C**uántos libros hay en esta página?

## los rotuladores
*rro-too-lah-DOR-es*
**felt-tip pens**

*Encuentra tu país en* **el globo**.

## el cuaderno de ejercicios
*koo'ah-DER-no deh eh-Hair-THI-thi-os*
**exercise book**

la cartera del colegio
school bag

## el globo
*GLO-bo*
**globe**

## los libros
*LEE-bros*
**books**

## el uniforme escolar
*oo-nee-FOR-meh ess-ko-LAR*
**school uniform**

## el ordenador
*or-den-ah-DOR*
**computer**

*The longest pencil in the world is almost 20 metres long.*

*School*

# Los deportes

## *Sports*

Llevo **un casco**.

el casco
helmet

el esquí
ski

**la raqueta**
*rrah-KEH-tah*
racket

**el ciclismo**
*thee-KLEES-mo*
cycling

la rueda
wheel

**el esquí**
*ess-KEE*
skiing

**el patinaje
sobre hielo**
*pah-tee-NAH-Heh
so-breh ee'EH-lo*
ice skating

**la gimnasia**
*Him-NAH-see-ah*
gymnastics

jugamos al baloncesto.

la camiseta
T-shirt

los pantalones
cortos
shorts

Eva quiere **marcar un gol**.

las zapatillas
trainers

**el baloncesto**
*bah-lon-THESS-to*
basketball

**el golf**
*golf*
golf

**el fútbol**
*FOOT-bol*
football

Hay alrededor de 28 deportes en los Juegos Olímpicos de verano.

Los deportes

**el atletismo**
*aht-leh-TISS-mo*
**athletics**

**el béisbol**
*BAY'ess-bol*
**baseball**

**el ejercicio**
*e-Her-THI-thi-o*
**exercise**

**el hockey**
*HO-kay*
**hockey**

**el hockey sobre hielo**
*HO-kay SO-breh e-EH-lo*
**ice hockey**

**el judo**
*HOO-do*
**judo**

**el kárate**
*KAH-rah-teh*
**karate**

**la natación**
*nah-tah-thi-ON*
**swimming**

¿**T**e gustan los deportes y el ejercicio?

la vela
sail

el bañador
trunks

**tirarse de cabeza**
*tee-RAH-seh deh kah-BEH-thah*
**diving**

**la vela**
*BEH-lah*
**sailing**

Levanto **los remos**.

el remo
oar

el balón
ball
el guante
glove

**el remo**
*RREH-mo*
**rowing**

el bote
boat

**el bate**
*BAH-teh*
**bat**

la raqueta
racket

el caballo
horse

**el rugby**
*RROOG-be*
**rugby**

**correr**
*kor-RRER*
**running**

**la equitación**
*eh-kee-tah-thi-ON*
**horse riding**

**el tenis**
*TEH-nees*
**tennis**

*There are about 28 sports in the summer Olympic Games.*

*Sports*

# Animales de compañía

## *Pets*

Animales de compañía

Mi cachorro se llama Honey.

la comida
food

el cuenco
bowl

**el cachorro**
*kah-CHOR-rro*
**puppy**

Una tortuga se mueve muy despacio.

**el hámster**
*AHM-stair*
**hamster**

**la tortuga**
*tor-TOO-gah*
**tortoise**

**el conejillo de indias**
*ko-neh-HE-yo deh IN-dee-ahs*
**guinea pig**

el collar
collar

**el conejo**
*ko-NEH-Ho*
**rabbit**

**¿Qué colores tiene el pelo del conejillo de indias?**

**el gato**
*GAH-to*
**cat**

**los peces dorados**
*PEH-thess do-RAH-dos*
**goldfish**

48    Un gato duerme alrededor de 16 horas al día.

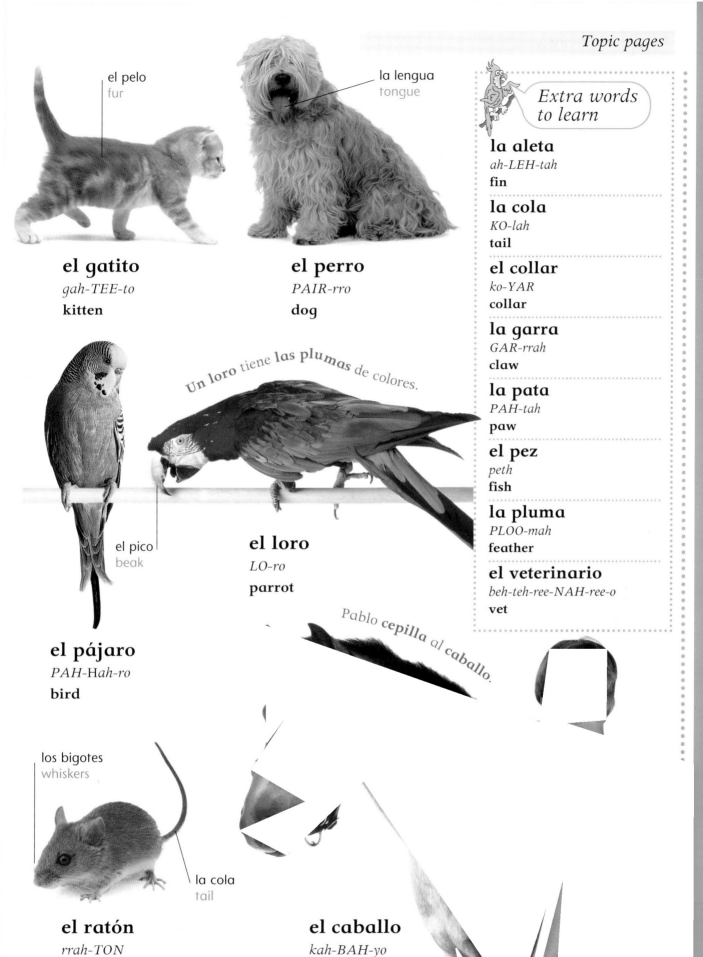

el pelo / fur

la lengua / tongue

**el gatito**
*gah-TEE-to*
**kitten**

**el perro**
*PAIR-rro*
**dog**

Un loro tiene las plumas de colores.

el pico / beak

**el loro**
*LO-ro*
**parrot**

**el pájaro**
*PAH-Hah-ro*
**bird**

Pablo cepilla al caballo.

los bigotes / whiskers

la cola / tail

**el ratón**
*rrah-TON*
**mouse**

**el caballo**
*kah-BAH-yo*
**horse**

*A cat sleeps about 16 hours a day.*

# Colores y formas
## Colours and shapes

**rojo**
*RRO-Ho*
red

**naranja**
*nah-rahn-Hah*
orange

**amarillo**
*ah-mah-REE-yo*
yellow

**verde**
*BAIR-deh*
green

**azul**
*ah-THOOL*
blue

**púrpura**
*POOR-poo-rah*
purple

**rosa**
*RRO-sah*
pink

**marrón**
*mah-RRON*
brown

**negro**
*NEH-gro*
black

curvo
curved

recto
straight

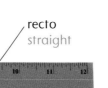

¿**C**uál es tu color y forma favoritos?

**50** Todos los colores son una mezcla de rojo, amarillo y azul.

**el cuadrado**
*koo'ah-DRAH-do*
square

**el círculo**
*THEER-koo-lo*
circle

el arco iris
rainbow

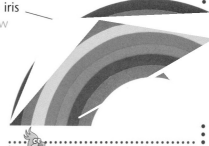

**el triángulo**
*tree-AHN-goo-lo*
triangle

**el rombo**
*RROM-bo*
diamond

**la estrella**
*ess-TREH-yah*
star

**el rectángulo**
*rrek-TAN-goo-lo*
rectangle

**el cubo**
*KOO-bo*
cube

**redondo**
*reh-DON-do*
round

*All colours are a mixture of red, yellow or blue.*

# Los contrarios
## Opposites

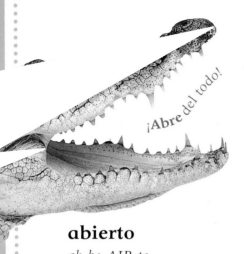

¡Abre del todo!

**abierto**
*ah-be-AIR-to*
open

**cerrado**
*thair-RRAH-do*
closed

**sucio**
*SOO-thi-o*
dirty

**áspero**
*AHS-peh-ro*
rough

**mojado**
*mo-HAH-do*
wet

**seco**
*seh-KO*
dry

**limpio**
*LIM-pee-o*
clean

**suave**
*soo'AH-beh*
smooth

> *Extra words to learn*

**lento**
*LEN-to*
slow

**ligero**
*lee-GEH-ro*
light

**lleno**
*YEH-no*
full

**nuevo**
*NOO'EH-bo*
new

**pesado**
*peh-SAH-do*
heavy

**rápido**
*RAH-pee-do*
fast

**vacío**
*bah-THI-o*
empty

**viejo**
*be-EH-Ho*
old

Los contrarios

¡La mayoría de las calabazas son naranja pero puedes plantarlas blancas y azules!

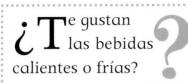

¿**T**e gustan las bebidas calientes o frías?

**frío**
*FREE-o*
**cold**

**caliente**
*kah-lee-EN-teh*
**hot**

*Una calabaza se pone **gorda** en otoño.*

**gordo**
*GOR-do*
**fat**

*Esta **verdura** es muy **delgada**.*

**delgado**
*del-GAH-do*
**thin**

**blando**
*BLAHN-do*
**soft**

**duro**
*DOO-ro*
**hard**

**bajo**
*bah-Ho*
**short**

**alto**
*ahl-to*
**tall**

**pequeño**
*peh-KEH-n'yo*
**small**

**grande**
*GRAHN-deh*
**big**

*Most pumpkins are orange, but you can grow white and blue ones!*

*Opposites*

**el muñeco de nieve**

*moo-N'YEH-ko deh
nee-EH-beh*

snowman

# El tiempo
## *Weather*

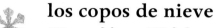

**los copos de nieve**

*KO-pos deh nee-EH-beh*

snowflakes

**el otoño**

*o-TO-n'yo*

autumn

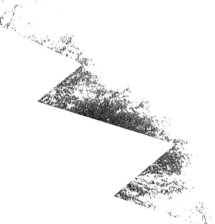

**la nieve**

*nee-EH-beh*

snow

**el gorro de lana**

*GOR-rro deh LAH-nah*

woolly hat

Me gustaría hacer **un muñeco de nieve.**

Llevo una bufanda y unos guantes.

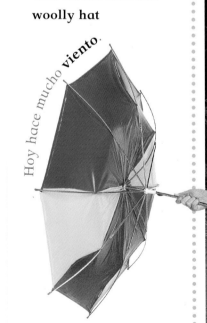

Hoy hace mucho **viento.**

**el paraguas**

*pah-RAH-goo'ahs*

umbrella

sun

El **sol** hace calor.

**la lluvia**
*YOO-be-ah*
rain

**la nube**
*NOO-beh*
cloud

**el arco iris**
*AR-ko EE-riss*
rainbow

**las gafas de sol**
*GAH-fahs deh sol*
sunglasses

**la gorra**
*GOR-rrah*
cap

55

# English A–Z

In this section English words are in alphabetical order, followed by the Spanish translation. There is information after each English word to show you what type of word it is. This will help you to make sentences. In Spanish, nouns (naming words) are either masculine (m) or feminine (f). If the Spanish word has *el* before it, it is masculine, if it has *la,* it is feminine.

(n) = noun (a naming word). Either masculine or feminine. Feminine nouns usually have an "a" at the end.

(adj) = adjective (a describing word). These words can change depending whether the noun they are describing is masculine or feminine.

(adv) = adverb (a word that gives more information about a verb, an adjective, or another adverb)

(conj) = conjunction (a joining word, e.g., and)

(prep) = preposition (e.g., about)

(pron) = pronoun (e.g., he, she, it)

(article) = (e.g., a, an, the)

(sing) = singular (one thing)   (plu) = plural (lots of things)

**apple**
la manzana

**a (article)**
un (m), una (f)
*oon/OO-nah*

**about (adv)**
aproximadamente
*ah-prok-se-mah-dah-MEN-teh*

**about (prep)**
de, sobre
*deh/SO-breh*

**above (prep)**
encima de
*en-THI-mah deh*

**accident (n)**
el accidente
*ack-thi-DEN-teh*

**across (prep)**
a través de
*ah-trah-BESS deh*

**activity (n)**
la actividad
*ack-tee-be-DAHD*

**address (n)**
la dirección
*dee-rek-thi-ON*

**adult (n)**
la adulta (f)
el adulto (m)
*ah-DOOL-tah/to*

**adventure (n)**
la aventura
*ah-ben-TOO-rah*

**aeroplane (n)**
el avión
*ah-be-ON*

**after (prep)**
después de
*dess-poo'ESS deh*

**afternoon (n)**
la tarde
*TAR-deh*

**again (adv)**
otra vez
*O-trah BETH*

**age (n)**
la edad
*eh-DAHD*

**air (n)**
el aire
*ΛH'E-reh*

**airport (n)**
el aeropuerto
*ah'eh-ro-poo'AIR-to*

**alarm clock (n)**
el despertador
*dess-pair-tah-DOOR*

**all (adj)**
todo
*TO-do*

**alligator (n)**
el caimán
*kah'e-MΛN*

**almost (adv)**
casi
*KAH-see*

**alone (adj)**
solo (m)
*SO-lo*

**alphabet (n)**
el alfabeto
*ahl-fah-BEH-to*

**already (adv)**
ya
*ya*

**also (adv)**
también
*tahm-be-EN*

**always (adv)**
siempre
*see-EM-preh*

**amazing (adj)**
increíble
*in-kreh-EE-bleh*

**ambulance (n)**
la ambulancia
*ahm-boo-LAN-thi-ah*

**an (article)**
un (m), una (f)
*oon/OO-nah*

**anchor (n)**
el ancla
*AHN-klah*

**and (conj)**
y or
e (before "i" or "hi")
*e*

**aeroplane**
el avión

**angry (adj)**
enfadado (m)
*en-fah-DAH-do*

**animal (n)**
el animal
*ahn-e-MAHL*

**ankle (n)**
el tobillo
*to-BE-yo*

**answer (n)**
la respuesta
*rress-POO´ESS-tah*

**ant (n)**
la hormiga
*or-MEE-gah*

**antenna (n)**
la antena
*ahn-TEH-nah*

**anybody (pron)**
alguien
*AHLG-e-en*

**anything (pron)**
algo
*AHL-go*

**apart (adv)**
separado
*seh-pah-RAH-do*

**apartment (n)**
el apartamento
*ah-par-tah-MEN-to*

**appearance (n)**
la apariencia
*ah-pah-ree-EN-thi-ah*

**apple (n)**
la manzana
*mahn-THAH-nah*

**apron (n)**
el mandil
*mahn-DEEL*

**arch (n)**
el arco
*AR-ko*

**area (n)**
el área
*AH-reh-ah*

**arm (n)**
el brazo
*BRAH-tho*

**armchair (n)**
el sillón
*see-YON*

**army (n)**
el ejército
*eh-HAIR-thi-to*

**around (prep)**
alrededor
*ahl-reh-deh-DOR*

**arrival (n)**
la llegada
*yeh-GAH-dah*

armchair
el sillón

astronaut
el astronauta

**arrow (n)**
la flecha
*FLEH-chah*

**art (n)**
el arte
*AR-teh*

**artist (n)**
el/la artista (m/f)
*ar-TISS-tah*

**assistant (n)**
el/la asistente (m/f)
*ah-siss-TEN-teh*

**astronaut (n)**
el/la astronauta (m/f)
*ahs-tro-NAH'OO-tah*

**astronomer (n)**
la astrónoma (f)
el astrónomo (m)
*ahs-TRO-no-mah/mo*

**athletics (n)**
el atletismo
*aht-leh-TISS-mo*

**atlas (n)**
el atlas
*AHT-lahs*

**attic (n)**
el ático
*AH-tee-ko*

**aunt (n)**
la tía
*TEE-ah*

**autumn (n)**
el otoño
*o-TO-n'yo*

**avocado (n)**
el aguacate
*ah-goo'ah-KAH-teh*

**away (adj)**
de fuera
*deh foo'EH-rah*

avocado
el aguacate

A
B
C
D
E
F
G
H
I
J
K
L
M
N
O
P
Q
R
S
T
U
V
W
X
Y
Z

# B

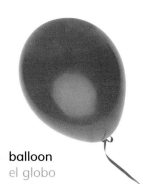

balloon
el globo

**baboon (n)**
el babuino
bah-boo-E'NO

**baby (n)**
el bebé
beh-BEH

**back (body) (n)**
la espalda
ess-PAHL-dah

**back (not front) (adj)**
parte de atrás
PAR-teh deh ah-TRAHS

**backpack (n)**
la mochila
mo-CHEE-lah

**backwards (adv)**
hacia atrás
AH-thi-ah ah-TRAHS

**bad (adj)**
malo (m)
MAH-lo

**badge (n)**
la chapa
CHAH-pah

**badminton (n)**
el bádminton
BAHD-min-ton

**bag (n)**
la bolsa
BOL-sah

**bakery (n)**
la panadería
pah-nah-deh-REE-ah

**balcony (n)**
el balcón
bahl-KON

**ball (n)**
el balón
bah-LON

**ballet dancer (n)**
el bailarín (m)
la bailarina (f)
bah'e-lah-REEN/ah

**balloon (n)**
el globo
GLO-bo

**banana (n)**
el plátano
PLAH-tah-no

**band (n)**
la banda
BAHN-dah

**bank (money) (n)**
el banco
BAHN-ko

**bank (river) (n)**
la orilla
o-REE-yah

**barbecue (n)**
la barbacoa
bar-bah-KO-ah

**barn (n)**
el granero
grah-NEH-ro

**baseball (n)**
el béisbol
BAY'ess-bol

**basket (n)**
la cesta
THESS-tah

**basketball (n)**
el baloncesto
bah-lon-THESS-to

**bat (animal) (n)**
el murciélago
moor-thi-EH-lah-go

**bat (sport) (n)**
el bate
BAH-teh

**bath (n)**
el baño
BAHN-n'yo

**bathroom (n)**
el cuarto de baño
koo'AR-to deh
BAHN-n'yo

**battery (n)**
la pila
PEE-lah

**battle (n)**
la batalla
bah-TAH-yah

**beach (n)**
la playa
PLAH-yah

bat
el murciélago

**bead (n)**
la cuenta
koo'EN-tah

**beak (n)**
el pico
PEE-ko

**beans (n)**
las alubias
ah-LOO-be-ahs

**bear (n)**
el oso
O-so

**beard (n)**
la barba
BAR-bah

**beautiful (adj)**
bello (m)
BEH-yo

**beauty (n)**
la belleza
beh-YEH-thah

**because (conj)**
porque
POR-keh

**bed (n)**
la cama
KAH-mah

**bedroom (n)**
la habitación
ah-be-tah-thi-ON

**bee (n)**
la abeja
ah-BEH-Hah

**beetle (n)**
el escarabajo
ess-kah-rah-BAH-Ho

bear
el oso

**before (prep)**
antes
*AHN-tes*

**behind (prep)**
detrás de
*deh-trahs deh*

**bell (metal) (n)**
la campana
*kahm-PAH-nah*

**below (prep)**
debajo de
*deh-BAH-Ho deh*

**belt (n)**
el cinturón
*thin-too-RON*

**bench (n)**
el banco
*BAHN-ko*

**best (pron)**
el/la mejor
*MEH-Hor*

**better (adj)**
mejor (sing)
mejores (plu)
*meh-HOR/meh-HOR-es*

**between (prep)**
entre
*EN-treh*

**big (adj)**
grande
*GRAHN-deh*

bike
la bici

saddle
el sillín

tyre
el neumático

wheel
la rueda

pedal
el pedal

binoculars
los prismáticos

**bike (n)**
la bici
*BE-thi*

**bill (n)**
la cuenta
*koo'EN-tah*

**billion**
billón
*be-YON*

**bin (rubbish) (n)**
el cubo de la basura
*KOO-bo deh lah*
*BAH-soo-rah*

**binoculars (n)**
los prismáticos
*priss-MAH-tee-kos*

**bird (n)**
el pájaro
*PAH-Hah-ro*

**bird-watching (n)**
la observación
de aves
*ob-sair-bah-thi-ON*
*deh AH-behs*

**birthday (n)**
el cumpleaños
*koom-pleh-AH-n'yos*

**birthday cake (n)**
la tarta de
cumpleaños
*TAR-tah deh*
*koom-pleh-AH-n'yos*

**birthday card (n)**
la tarjeta de
cumpleaños
*tar-HEH-tah deh*
*koom-pleh-AH-n'yos*

**biscuit (n)**
la galleta
*gah-YEH-tah*

**black (adj)**
negro (m)
*NEH-gro*

**blackboard (n)**
la pizarra
*pee-THAR-rrah*

**blanket (n)**
la manta
*MAHN-tah*

**blind (adj)**
ciego (m)
*thi-EH-go*

**blonde (adj)**
rubio (m)
*RROO-be-oh*

**blood (n)**
la sangre
*SAHN-greh*

**blouse (n)**
la blusa
*BLOO-sah*

**blue (adj)**
azul
*ah-THOOL*

**board (n)**
la tabla
*TAH-blah*

**board game (n)**
el juego de mesa
*Hoo'AY-go deh MEH-sah*

B

A C D E F G H I J K L M N O P Q R S T U V W X Y Z

**boat (n)**
el bote
*BO-teh*

**body (n)**
el cuerpo
*koo'ER-po*

**bone (n)**
el hueso
*oo'EH-so*

**book (n)**
el libro
*LEE-bro*

**bookshop (n)**
la librería
*lee-breh-REE-ah*

**boot (n)**
la bota
*BO-tah*

**boring (adj)**
aburrido
*ah-boo-RREE-do*

**bottle (n)**
la botella
*bo-TEH-yah*

**bottom (n)**
el fondo
*FON-do*

**bowl (n)**
el cuenco
*koo'EN-ko*

**box (n)**
la caja
*KAH-Hah*

**boy (n)**
el niño
*NEE-n'yo*

**boyfriend (n)**
el novio
*NO-be-oh*

**bracelet (n)**
el brazalete
*brah-thah-LEH-teh*

**brain (n)**
el cerebro
*theh-REH-bro*

**branch (n)**
la rama
*RRAH-mah*

**brave (adj)**
valiente
*bah-lee-EN-teh*

**bread (n)**
el pan
*pahn*

**break (n)**
el descanso
*dess-KAN-so*

**breakfast (n)**
el desayuno
*deh-sah-YOO-no*

**breeze (n)**
la brisa
*BREE-sah*

**bridge (n)**
el puente
*poo'EN-teh*

**bright (adj)**
brillante
*bree-YAHN-teh*

bubbles
las burbujas

butterfly
la mariposa

**broccoli (n)**
el brécol
*BREH-kol*

**broken (adj)**
roto (m)
*RRO-to*

**broom (n)**
la escoba
*ess-KO-bah*

**brother (n)**
el hermano
*air-MAH-no*

**brown (adj)**
marrón
*mah-RRON*

**bubble (n)**
la burbuja
*boor-BOO-Hah*

**bucket (n)**
el cubo
*KOO-boh*

**buggy (n)**
el cochecito
*ko-cheh-THI-to*

**building (n)**
el edificio
*eh-dee-fee-THI-o*

**bulb (light) (n)**
la bombilla
*bom-BEE-yah*

**bulb (plant) (n)**
el bulbo
*BOOL-bo*

**buoy (n)**
la boya
*BO-yah*

**bus (n)**
el autobús
*ah'oo-to-BOOS*

**bus stop (n)**
la parada de
autobús
*pah-RAH-dah deh
ah'oo-to-BOOS*

**bush (n)**
el arbusto
*ar-BOOS-to*

**business (n)**
el negocio
*neh-GO-thi-o*

**busy (adj)**
ocupado (m)
*o-koo-PAH-do*

**but (conj)**
pero
*PEH-ro*

**butter (n)**
la mantequilla
*mahn-teh-KEE-yah*

**butterfly (n)**
la mariposa
*mah-ree-PO-sah*

**button (n)**
el botón
*bo-TON*

# C

cake
el pastel

**cabbage (n)**
el repollo
*rreh-PO-yo*

**cactus (n)**
el cáctus
*KAHK-tooss*

**café (n)**
la cafetería
*kah-feh-teh-REE-ah*

**cage (n)**
la jaula
*Hah'OO-lah*

**cake (n)**
el pastel
*pahs-TEL*

**calculator (n)**
la calculadora
*kahl-koo-lah-DOR-ah*

**calendar (n)**
el calendario
*kah-len-DAH-ree-o*

**calf (n)**
el ternero
*tair-NEH-ro*

**calm (adj)**
tranquilo (m)
*tran-KEE-lo*

**camel (n)**
el camello
*kah-MEH-yo*

**camera (n)**
la cámara
*KAH-mah-rah*

**can (n)**
el bote
*BO-teh*

**candle (n)**
la vela
*BEH-lah*

**canoe (n)**
la canoa
*kah-NO-ah*

**cap (n)**
la gorra
*GOR-rrah*

**capital (n)**
la capital
*kah-pee-TAHL*

**car (n)**
el coche
*KO-cheh*

**card (n)**
la tarjeta
*tar-HEH-tah*

**cardboard (n)**
el cartón
*kar-TON*

**cards (n)**
las cartas
*KAR-tahs*

**careful (adj)**
cuidadoso (m)
*koo'e-dah-DO-so*

**carpet (n)**
la moqueta
*mo-KEH-tah*

**carrot (n)**
la zanahoria
*thah-nah-O-ree-yah*

**cart (n)**
el carro
*KAR-rro*

**cash (n)**
el dinero
(en efectivo)
*dee-NEH-ro
(en eh-fek-TEE-bo)*

**cassette (n)**
la cinta
*THIN-tah*

**cat (n)**
el gato
*GAH-to*

**caterpillar (n)**
la oruga
*o-ROO-gah*

**cave (n)**
la cueva
*koo'EH-bah*

**CD (n)**
el CD
*theh-DEH*

**CD player (n)**
el reproductor
de CD
*rreh-pro-dook-TOR
deh theh-DEH*

**ceiling (n)**
el techo
*TEH-cho*

**cellar (n)**
el sótano
*SO-tah-no*

**centre (n)**
el centro
*THEN-tro*

**cereal (n)**
los cereales
*theh-reh-AHL-ess*

**chain (n)**
la cadena
*kah-DEH-nah*

**chair (n)**
la silla
*SEE-yah*

**challenge (n)**
el desafío
*deh-sah-FEE-o*

**change (n)**
el cambio
*KAHM-be-o*

**cheap (adj)**
barato (m)
*bah-RAH-to*

**checkout (n)**
la caja
*KAH-Hah*

**cheese (n)**
el queso
*KEH-so*

**cheetah (n)**
el guepardo
*goo'eh-PAR-do*

car
el coche

door
la puerta

A B C D E F G H I J K L M N O P Q R S T U V W X Y Z

**C**

**chef (n)**
el/la chef (m/f)
*CHEH-feh*

**chemist (shop) (n)**
la farmacia
*far-MAH-thi-ah*

**chess (n)**
el ajedrez
*ah-Heh-DRETH*

**chest (body) (n)**
el pecho
*PEH-cho*

**chest of drawers (n)**
la cómoda
*KO-mo-dah*

**chewing gum (n)**
el chicle
*CHEE-kleh*

**chick (n)**
el pollito
*po-YEE-to*

**chicken (n)**
el pollo
*PO-yo*

**child (n)**
la niña (f)
el niño (m)
*NEE-n'yah/n'yo*

**children (n)**
los niños
*NEE-n'yoss*

computer
el ordenador

**chimney (n)**
la chimenea
*chee-meh-NEH-ah*

**chimpanzee (n)**
el chimpancé
*chim-pahn-THEH*

**chin (n)**
la barbilla
*bar-BE-yah*

**chips (n)**
las patatas fritas
*pah-TAH-tass*
*FREE-tass*

**chocolate (n)**
el chocolate
*cho-ko-LAH-teh*

**Christmas (n)**
las navidades
*nah-be-DAH-dess*

**church (n)**
la iglesia
*e-GLEH-see-ah*

**cinema (n)**
el cine
*THI-neh*

**circle (n)**
el círculo
*THEER-koo-lo*

**circus (n)**
el circo
*THEER-ko*

**city (n)**
la ciudad
*thi-oo-DAHD*

**classroom (n)**
el aula
*ah'OO-lah*

**claw (n)**
la garra
*GAR-rrah*

**clean (adj)**
limpio (m)
*LIM-pee-o*

**clear (adj)**
claro (m)
*KLAH-ro*

**clever (adj)**
listo (m)
*LISS-to*

**cliff (n)**
el acantilado
*ah-kahn-tee-LAH-do*

**cloak (n)**
la capa
*KAH-pah*

**clock (n)**
el reloj
*rreh-LOH*

**close (adj)**
cerca
*THAIR-kah*

**closed (adj)**
cerrado (m)
*thair-RRAH-do*

**cloth (n)**
la tela
*TEH-lah*

**clothes (n)**
la ropa
*RRO-pah*

**cloud (n)**
la nube
*NOO-beh*

**cloudy (adj)**
nublado (m)
*noo-BLAH-do*

**clown (n)**
el payaso
*pah-YAH-so*

**coach (n)**
el autobús
*ah'oo-to-BOOS*

**coast (n)**
la costa
*KOSS-tah*

**coat (n)**
el abrigo
*ah-BREE-go*

**coat hanger (n)**
la percha
*PER-chah*

**coconut (n)**
el coco
*KO-ko*

**coffee (n)**
el café
*kah-FEH*

**coin (n)**
la moneda
*mo-NEH-dah*

**cold (adj)**
frío (m)
*FREE-o*

**collar (n)**
el collar
*ko-YAR*

**collecting (n)**
el coleccionismo
*ko-lek-thi-o-NISS-mo*

**college (n)**
el colegio
*ko-LEH-He-o*

**colour (n)**
el color
*ko-LOR*

**coloured pencil (n)**
el lápiz de color
*LAH-pith deh ko-LOR*

**colourful (adj)**
colorido (m)
*ko-lo-REE-do*

hard drive
el disco duro

keyboard | screen
el teclado | la pantalla

mouse mat | mouse
la alfombrilla | el ratón

compass
la brújula

**comb (n)**
el peine
*PEH'eh-neh*

**combine harvester (n)**
la cosechadora
*ko-seh-chah-DOO-rah*

**comfortable (adj)**
cómodo (m)
*KO-mo-do*

**comic (n)**
el tebeo
*teh-BEH-o*

**compass (n)**
la brújula
*BROO-Hoo-lah*

**computer (n)**
el ordenador
*or-den-ah-DOR*

**computer game (n)**
el videojuego
*be-deh-o-Hoo'EH-go*

**concert (n)**
el concierto
*kon-thi-AIR-to*

crab
el cangrejo

**continent (n)**
el continente
*kon-tee-NEN-teh*

**controls (n)**
los mandos
*MAHN-dos*

**cooker (n)**
la cocina
*ko-THI-nah*

**cooking (n)**
la cocina
*ko-THI-nah*

**cool (adj)**
fresco (m)
*FRESS-ko*

**coral reef (n)**
el arrecife de coral
*ar-rreh-THI-feh deh ko-RAHL*

**cork (n)**
el corcho
*KOR-cho*

**corner (n)**
la esquina
*ess-KEE-nah*

**correct (adj)**
correcto (m)
*kor-RREK-to*

**costume (n)**
el traje
*TRAH-Heh*

**cotton (n)**
el algodón
*ahl-go-DON*

**cough (n)**
la tos
*toss*

**country (n)**
el país
*pah'ISS*

**countryside (n)**
el campo
*KAHM-po*

**cousin (n)**
la prima (f)
el primo (m)
*PREE-mah/mo*

**cow (n)**
la vaca
*BAH-kah*

**cowboy (n)**
el vaquero
*bah-KEH-ro*

**crab (n)**
el cangrejo
*kahn-GREH-Ho*

**crane (n)**
la grúa
*GROO'ah*

**crayon (n)**
la cera
*THEH-rah*

**cream (food) (n)**
la nata
*NAH-tah*

**creature (n)**
la criatura
*kree-ah-TOO-rah*

**crew (n)**
la tripulación
*tree-poo-lah-thi-ON*

**crocodile (n)**
el cocodrilo
*ko-ko-DREE-lo*

**crop (n)**
la cosecha
*ko-SEH-chah*

**crossing (n)**
el cruce
*KROO-theh*

**crowded (adj)**
abarrotado (m)
*ah-bar-rroh-TAH-do*

**crown (n)**
la corona
*ko-RO-nah*

**cube (n)**
el cubo
*KOO-bo*

**cup (n)**
la taza
*TAH-thah*

**cupboard (n)**
el armario
*ar-MAH-ree-o*

**curious (adj)**
curioso (m)
*koo-ree-O-so*

**curly (adj)**
rizado (m)
*ree-THAH-do*

**curtain (n)**
la cortina
*kor-TEE-nah*

**curved (adj)**
curvo (m)
*KOR-bo*

**cushion (n)**
el cojín
*ko-HEEN*

**customer (n)**
el/la cliente (m/f)
*klee-EN-teh*

**cycling (n)**
el ciclismo
*thee-KLEES-mo*

crown
la corona

# D

daisy
la margarita

**dad (n)**
el papá
pah-PAH

**dairy (products) (n)**
los productos lácteos
pro-DOOK-tos LAK-teh-os

**daisy (n)**
la margarita
mar-gah-REE-tah

**dam (n)**
la presa
PREH-sah

**dancer (n)**
el bailarín (m)
la bailarina (f)
bah'e-lah-REEN/ah

**dancing (n)**
el baile
BAH'e-leh

**dandelion (n)**
el diente de león
dee-EN-teh deh lee-ON

**danger (n)**
el peligro
peh-LEE-gro

**dangerous (adj)**
peligroso (m)
peh-lee-GRO-so

**dark (adj)**
oscuro (m)
oss-KOO-ro

**date (n)**
la fecha
FEH-chah

**daughter (n)**
la hija
EE-Hah

**day (n)**
el día
DEE-ah

**dead (adj)**
muerto (m)
moo-AIR-to

**deaf (adj)**
sordo (m)
SOR-do

**dear (letter) (adj)**
querido (m)
keh-REE-do

**deck chair (n)**
la tumbona
toom-BO-nah

**decorations (n)**
los adornos
ah-DOR-nos

**deep (adj)**
profundo (m)
pro-FOON-do

**deer (n)**
el ciervo
thi-AIR-bo

**delicious (adj)**
delicioso (m)
deh-lee-thi-O-so

**dentist (n)**
el/la dentista (m/f)
den-TEES-tah

**desert (n)**
el desierto
deh-see-AIR-to

**desk (n)**
el escritorio
ess-kree-TO-ree-o

**dessert (n)**
el postre
POSS-treh

**diagram (n)**
el diagrama
dee-ah-GRAH-mah

**diamond (n)**
el rombo
RRHOM-bo

**diary (n)**
la agenda
ah-HEN-dah

**dice (n)**
el dado
DAH-do

**dictionary (n)**
el diccionario
dik-thi-o-NAH-ree-o

**different (adj)**
diferente
dee-feh-REN-teh

**difficult (adj)**
difícil
dee-FEE-thil

**digital (adj)**
digital
dee-He-TAHL

**dining room (n)**
el comedor
koh-meh-DOR

**dinner (n)**
la cena
THEH-nah

**dinosaur (n)**
el dinosaurio
dee-no-SAH'oo-ree-o

**direction (n)**
la dirección
dee-rek-thi-ON

**directly (adj)**
directamente
dee-rek-tah-MEN-teh

**dirty (adj)**
sucio (m)
SOO-thi-o

**disabled (adj)**
discapacitado (m)
diss-kah-pah-thi-TAH-do

**disco (n)**
la discoteca
diss-ko-TEH-kah

**discovery (n)**
el descubrimiento
dess-koo-bree-ME'EN-to

**distance (n)**
la distancia
diss-TAN-thi-ah

**divorced (adj)**
divorciado (m)
dee-bor-THI-AH-do

**doctor (n)**
la médica (f)
el médico (m)
MEH-dee-kah/ko

**dog (n)**
el perro
PAIR-rro

**doll (n)**
la muñeca
moo-N'YEH-kah

**dolphin (n)**
el delfín
del-FEEN

**dome (n)**
la cúpula
KOO-poo-lah

**door (n)**
la puerta
poo-AIR-tah

**dormouse (n)**
el lirón
lee-RON

**downstairs (adv)**
abajo
ah-BAH-Ho

**dragon (n)**
el dragón
drah-GON

**dragonfly (n)**
la libélula
lee-BEH-loo-lah

**drawer (n)**
el cajón
*kah-HON*

**drawing (n)**
el dibujo
*dee-BOO-Ho*

**drawing pin (n)**
la chincheta
*cheen-CHEH-tah*

**dream (n)**
el sueño
*soo'EH-n'yo*

**dress (n)**
el vestido
*bess-TEE-do*

**drink (n)**
la bebida
*beh-BEE-dah*

**drop (n)**
la gota
*GOH-tah*

**drum (n)**
el tambor
*tahm-BOR*

**drum kit (n)**
la batería
*bah-teh-REE-ah*

**dry (adj)**
seco (m)
*seh-KO*

**duck (n)**
el pato
*PAH-to*

**duckling (n)**
el patito
*pah-TEE-to*

**during (prep)**
durante
*doo-RAHN-teh*

**dust (n)**
el polvo
*POL-bo*

**duvet (n)**
el edredón
*eh-dreh-DON*

**DVD (n)**
el DVD
*deh-oo-beh-DEH*

**DVD player (n)**
el reproductor
de DVD
*rreh-pro-dook-TOR
deh-oo-beh-DEH*

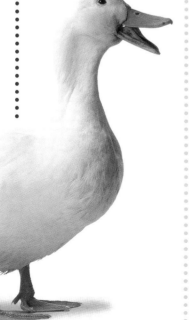

duck
el pato

# E

egg
el huevo

**each (adj)**
cada
*KAH-dah*

**eagle (n)**
el águila
*AH-ghee-lah*

**ear (n)**
la oreja
*o-REH-Hah*

**earache (n)**
el dolor de oídos
*do-LOR deh o'EE-dohs*

**early (adv)**
temprano
*tem-PRAH-no*

**earring (n)**
el pendiente
*pen-dee-EN-teh*

**Earth (planet) (n)**
la Tierra
*tee-AIR-rrah*

**earthworm (n)**
la lombriz
*lom-BREETH*

**east (n)**
el este
*ESS-teh*

**easy (adj)**
fácil
*FAH-thil*

**echo (n)**
el eco
*EH-ko*

**edge (n)**
el borde
*BOR-deh*

**effect (n)**
el efecto
*eh-FEK-to*

**egg (n)**
el huevo
*oo'EH-bo*

**elbow (n)**
el codo
*KO-do*

**electrical (adj)**
eléctrico (m)
*eh-LEH-tree-ko*

**elephant (n)**
el elefante
*eh-leh-FAN-teh*

**email (n)**
el correo
electrónico
*ko-RREH-o
eh-lek-TRO-nee-ko*

**email address (n)**
la dirección
electrónica
*dee-rek-thi-ON
eh-lek-TRO-nee-kah*

**emergency (n)**
la emergencia
*eh-mair-HEN-thi-ah*

**empty (adj)**
vacío (m)
*bah-THI-o*

**encyclopedia (n)**
la enciclopedia
*en-thi-klo-PEH-dee-ah*

**end (n)**
el fin
*fin*

**A B C D E F G H I J K L M N O P Q R S T U V W X Y Z**

**English (n)**
el inglés
*in-GLEHS*

**enough (adj)**
suficiente
*soo-fee-thi-EN-teh*

**enthusiastic (adj)**
entusiasta
*en-too-see-AHS-tah*

**entrance (n)**
la entrada
*en-TRAH-dah*

**envelope (n)**
el sobre
*SO-breh*

**environment (n)**
el medio ambiente
*MEH-dee-o
ahm-be-EN-teh*

**equal (adj)**
igual
*e-goo'AHL*

**equator (n)**
el ecuador
*eh-koo'AH-dor*

**equipment (n)**
el equipo
*eh-KEE-po*

**even (adv)**
incluso
*in-KLOO-so*

**evening (n)**
la tarde noche
*TAR-deh NO-cheh*

**event (n)**
el evento
*e-BEN-to*

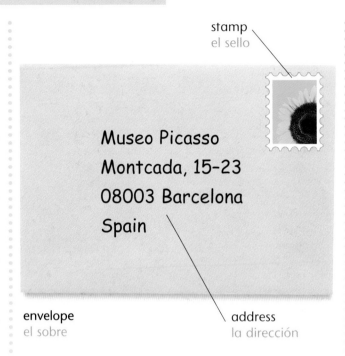

stamp
el sello

Museo Picasso
Montcada, 15–23
08003 Barcelona
Spain

envelope
el sobre

address
la dirección

**every (adj)**
cada
*KAH-dah*

**everybody (pron)**
todo el mundo
*TO-do ell MOON-do*

**everything (pron)**
todo
*TO-do*

**everywhere (adv)**
en todas partes
*en TO-dahs PAR-tess*

**exam (n)**
el exámen
*ek-SAH-men*

**excellent (adj)**
excelente
*eks-theh-LEN-teh*

**exchange (n)**
el cambio
*KAHM-be-o*

**excited (adj)**
emocionado (m)
*eh-mo-thi-o-NAH-do*

**exercise (n)**
el ejercicio
*e-Her-THI-thi-o*

**exercise bike (n)**
la bicicleta estática
*be-thi-KLEH-tah
ess-TAH-tee-kah*

**exercise book (n)**
el cuaderno de
ejercicios
*koo'ah-DER-no deh
eh-Hair-THI-thi-os*

**expedition (n)**
la expedición
*eks-peh-dee-thi-ON*

exercise
el ejercicio

**expensive (adj)**
caro
*KAH-ro*

**experiment (n)**
el experimento
*eks-peh-ree-MEN-to*

**expert (n)**
la experta (f)
el experto (m)
*eks-PAIR-tah/to*

**explorer (n)**
el explorador (m)
la exploradora (f)
*eks-plo-rah-DOR/ah*

**explosion (n)**
la explosión
*eks-plo-see-ON*

**extinct (adj)**
extinto (m)
*eks-TIN-to*

**extra (adj)**
de más
*deh mahs*

**extremely (adv)**
extremadamente
*eks-treh-mah-dah-
MEN-teh*

**eye (n)**
el ojo
*o-Ho*

**eyebrow (n)**
la ceja
*THEH-Hah*

**eyelash (n)**
la pestaña
*pess-TAH-n'yah*

arm
el brazo

hand
la mano

leg
la pierna

foot
el pie

# F

fancy dress
el disfraz

**fabulous (adj)**
fabuloso (m)
*fah-boo-LO-so*

**face (n)**
la cara
*KAH-rah*

**fact (n)**
el hecho
*EH-cho*

**factory (n)**
la fábrica
*FAH-bree-kah*

**faint (pale) (adj)**
borroso (m)
*bor-RRO-so*

**fair (n)**
la feria
*FEH-ree-ah*

**false (adj)**
falso (m)
*FAHL-so*

**family (n)**
la familia
*fah-MEE-lee-ah*

**famous (adj)**
famoso (m)
*fah-MO-so*

**fancy dress (n)**
el disfraz
*diss-FRATH*

**fantastic (adj)**
fantástico (m)
*fan-TASS-tee-ko*

**far (adv)**
lejos
*LEH-Hos*

**farm (n)**
la granja
*GRAHN-Hah*

**farmer (n)**
el agricultor (m)
la agricultora (f)
*ah-gree-kool-TOR/ah*

**fashion (n)**
la moda
*MO-dah*

**fashionable (adj)**
de moda
*deh MO-dah*

**fast (adv)**
rápido
*RAH-pee-do*

**fat (adj)**
gordo (m)
*GOR-do*

**father (n)**
el padre
*PAH-dreh*

**favourite (adj)**
favorito (m)
*fah-bo-REE-to*

**feather (n)**
la pluma
*PLOO-mah*

**felt (n)**
el fieltro
*fee'ELL-troh*

**felt-tip pen (n)**
el rotulador
*rro-too-lah-DOR*

**female (n)**
la mujer
*MOO-Hair*

**fence (n)**
la valla
*BAH-yah*

**fern (n)**
el helecho
*eh-LEH-cho*

**ferry (n)**
el ferry
*FEH-rree*

**festival (n)**
el festival
*fess-tee-BAHL*

**field (n)**
el prado
*PRAH-do*

**film (n)**
la película
*peh-LEE-koo-lah*

**film star (n)**
la estrella de cine
*ess-TREH-yah
deh THI-neh*

**fin (n)**
la aleta
*ah-LEH-tah*

**fine (adv)**
bien
*be-EN*

**finger (n)**
el dedo
*DEH-do*

**fire (n)**
el fuego
*foo'EH-go*

**fire engine (n)**
el coche de
bomberos
*KOH-cheh deh
bom-BEH-rohs*

**firefighter (n)**
la bombera
el bombero
*bom-BEH-rah/ro*

**first (adv)**
primero
*pree-MEH-ro*

**first aid (n)**
los primeros auxilios
*pree-MEH-rohs
ah'ook-SEE-lee-ohs*

**fish (n)**
el pez
*peth*

**fishing (n)**
la pesca
*PESS-kah*

**fishing boat (n)**
el barco de pesca
*BAR-ko deh PESS-kah*

**fishing line (n)**
el sedal
*seh-DAHL*

**fist (n)**
el puño
*POO-n'yo*

eye
el ojo

fin
la aleta

fish
el pez

A B C D E **F** G H I J K L M N O P Q R S T U V W X Y Z

A B C D E **F** G H I J K L M N O P Q R S T U V W X Y Z

football
el balón de fútbol

**fit (adj)**
en forma
*en FOR-mah*

**flag (n)**
la bandera
*bahn-DEH-rah*

**flannel (n)**
la toallita
*to-ah-YEE-tah*

**flat (adj)**
llano (m)
*YAH-no*

**flats (building) (n)**
el bloque de pisos
*BLO-keh deh PEE-sos*

**fleece (jacket) (n)**
el forro polar
*FOR-rro po-LAR*

**flesh (n)**
la carne
*KAR-neh*

**flipper (n)**
la aleta
*ah-LEH-tah*

**flock (n)**
el rebaño
*rre-BAH-n'yo*

**flood (n)**
la inundación
*in-oon-dah-thi-ON*

**floor (n)**
el suelo
*soo'EH-lo*

**flour (n)**
la harina
*ah-REE-nah*

**flower (n)**
la flor
*flor*

**flowerpot (n)**
la maceta
*mah-THEH-tah*

**flute (n)**
la flauta
*FLAH'oo-tah*

**fly (n)**
la mosca
*MOSS-kah*

**fog (n)**
la niebla
*nee-EH-blah*

**food (n)**
la comida
*ko-MEE-dah*

**foot (n)**
el pie
*PEE-eh*

**football (ball) (n)**
el balón de fútbol
*bah-LON deh FOOT-bol*

**football (game) (n)**
el fútbol
*FOOT-bol*

**for (prep)**
para
*PAH-rah*

**foreign (adj)**
extranjero (m)
*eks-trahn-HEH-ro*

**forest (n)**
el bosque
*BOSS-keh*

**fork (n)**
el tenedor
*teh-neh-DOR*

**forward (adv)**
adelante
*ah-deh-LAN-teh*

**fossil (n)**
el fósil
*FO-sil*

**fox (n)**
el zorro
*THO-rro*

**frame (n)**
el marco
*MAR-ko*

**free time (n)**
el tiempo libre
*tee-EM-po LEE-breh*

**freezer (n)**
el congelador
*kon-Heh-lah-DOR*

**French (n)**
el francés
*fran-THESS*

**fresh (adj)**
fresco (m)
*FRESS-ko*

**fridge (n)**
el frigorífico
*free-go-REE-fee-ko*

**friend (n)**
la amiga (f)
el amigo (m)
*ah-mee-gah/go*

**friendly (adj)**
simpático (m)
*sim-PAH-tee-ko*

**frightened (adj)**
asustado (m)
*ah-soos-tah-do*

**frightening (adj)**
espantoso (m)
*ess-pahn-TO-so*

**frog (n)**
la rana
*RRAH-nah*

**from (prep)**
de
*deh*

**front door (n)**
la puerta principal
*poo'ER-tah prin-thi-PAHL*

**fruit (n)**
la fruta
*FROO-tah*

**frying pan (n)**
la sartén
*sar-TEN*

**fuel (n)**
el combustible
*kom-booss-TEE-bleh*

**full (adj)**
lleno (m)
*YEH-no*

**fun (n)**
la diversión
*dee-bair-see-ON*

**fur (n)**
el pelo
*PEH-lo*

**furniture (n)**
los muebles
*moo'EH-blehs*

**future (n)**
el futuro
*foo-TOO-ro*

frog
la rana

# G

globe
el globo

**game (n)**
el juego
Hoo'EH-go

**garage (n)**
el garaje
gah-RAH-Heh

**garden (n)**
el jardín
Har-DEEN

**gardener (n)**
la jardinera (f)
el jardinero (m)
Har-dee-NEH-rah/ro

**gardening (n)**
la jardinería
Har-dee-neh-REE-ah

**gas (n)**
el gas
gahs

**gentle (adj)**
dulce
DOOL-theh

**German (n)**
el alemán
ah-leh-MAHN

**giant (n)**
el gigante
He-GAHN-teh

**giraffe (n)**
la jirafa
He-RAH-fah

**girl (n)**
la niña
NEE-n'yah

**girlfriend (n)**
la novia
NO-be-ah

**glass (drink) (n)**
el vaso
BAH-so

**glasses (n)**
las gafas
GAH-fahs

**globe (n)**
el globo
GLO-bo

**glove (n)**
el guante
goo'AN-teh

**glue (n)**
el pegamento
peh-gah-MEN-to

**goal (n)**
el gol
gol

**goat (n)**
la cabra
KAH-brah

**God (n)**
el Dios
dee-OSS

**goggles (n)**
las gafas de nadar
GAH-fahs deh nah-DAR

**gold (n)**
el oro
O-ro

**goldfish (n)**
el pez dorado
peth do-RAH-do

**golf (n)**
el golf
golf

**good (adj)**
bueno (m)
boo'EH-no

**gorilla (n)**
el gorila
goh-REE-lah

**government (n)**
el gobierno
go-be-AIR-no

**grandfather (n)**
el abuelo
ah-boo'EH-lo

**grandmother (n)**
la abuela
ah-boo'EH-lah

**grandparents (n)**
los abuelos
ah-boo'EH-los

**grape (n)**
la uva
OO-bah

**grass (n)**
el césped
THESS-ped

**grasshopper (n)**
el saltamontes
sahl-tah-MON-tess

**great (good) (adj)**
estupendo (m)
ess-too-PEN-do

**green (adj)**
verde
BAIR-deh

**greenhouse (n)**
el invernadero
in-bair-nah-DEH-ro

**ground (n)**
el suelo
la tierra
soo'EH-lo/tee-AIR-rrah

**group (n)**
el grupo
GROO-po

**guide (n)**
la guía
GHEE-ah

**guinea pig (n)**
el conejillo
de indias
ko-neh-HE-yo
deh IN-dee-ahs

**guitar (n)**
la guitarra
ghee-TAH-rah

**gymnastics (n)**
la gimnasia
Him-NAH-see-ah

guitar
la guitarra

A
B
C
D
E
F
**G**
H
I
J
K
L
M
N
O
P
Q
R
S
T
U
V
W
X
Y
Z

# H

handbag
el bolso

**habitat (n)**
el hábitat
*AH-be-tat*

**hair (n)**
el pelo
*PEH-lo*

**hairbrush (n)**
el cepillo del pelo
*theh-PEE-yo del PEH-lo*

**hairdresser's (n)**
la peluquería
*peh-loo-keh-REE-ah*

hat
el sombrero

---

**hairy (adj)**
peludo (m)
*peh-LOO-do*

**half (n)**
la mitad
*mee-TAHD*

**hall (n)**
el recibidor
*reh-thi-be-DOR*

**hamster (n)**
el hámster
*AHM-stair*

**hand (n)**
la mano
*MAH-no*

**handbag (n)**
el bolso
*BOL-so*

**handkerchief (n)**
el pañuelo
*pah-n'yoo-EH-lo*

**hang-glider (n)**
el ala delta
*AH-lah DEL-tah*

**happy (adj)**
feliz
*feh-LEETH*

**harbour (n)**
el puerto
*poo'ER-to*

**hard (adj)**
duro (m)
*DOO-ro*

---

**hard drive (n)**
el disco duro
*DISS-ko DOO-ro*

**hare (n)**
la liebre
*lee-EH-breh*

**harvest (n)**
la cosecha
*ko-SEH-chah*

**hat (n)**
el sombrero
*som-BREH-ro*

**hawk (n)**
el halcón
*ahl-KON*

**hay (n)**
la paja
*PAH-Hah*

**he (n)**
él
*ell*

**head (n)**
la cabeza
*kah-BEH-thah*

**headache (n)**
el dolor de cabeza
*do-LOR deh*
*kah-BEH-thah*

**healthy (adj)**
sano (m)
*SAH-no*

**heart (n)**
el corazón
*ko-rah-THON*

**heat (n)**
el calor
*kah-LOR*

**heavy (adj)**
pesado (m)
*peh-SAH-do*

**helicopter (n)**
el helicóptero
*eh-lee-KOP-teh-ro*

---

hamster
el hámster

**helmet (n)**
el casco
*KAHS-ko*

**help (n)**
la ayuda
*ah-YOO-dah*

**her (adj)**
su (sing), sus (plu)
*soo/soos*

**her (pron)**
la, le
*lah/leh*

**hero (n)**
el héroe
*EH-ro-eh*

**heron (n)**
la garza real
*GAR-thah rreh-AHL*

**hers (pron)**
suya (f)
suyo (m)
suyas (f plu)
suyos (m plu)
*SOO-ya/yo/yahs/yos*

**hi**
hola
*O-lah*

**hide-and-seek (n)**
el escondite
*ess-kon-DEE-teh*

**high (adj)**
alto (m)
*AHL-to*

**hill (n)**
la colina
ko-LEE-nah

**him (pron)**
le, lo
leh/lo

**hip (n)**
la cadera
kah-DEH-rah

**his (adj)**
su (sing), sus (plu)
soo/soos

**his (pron)**
suya (f)
suyo (m)
suyas (f plu)
suyos (m plu)
SOO-ya/yo/yahs/yos

**historical (adj)**
histórico (m)
iss-TO-ree-ko

**history (n)**
la historia
iss-TO-ree-ah

**hive (n)**
la colmena
kohl-MEH-nah

**hobby (n)**
el hobby
HO-be

**hockey (n)**
el hockey
HO-kay

**hole (n)**
el agujero
ah-goo-HEH-ro

**holiday (n)**
las vacaciones
bah-kah-thi-O-ness

**home (n)**
la casa
KAH-sah

**homework (n)**
los deberes
deh-BEH-ress

**honey (n)**
la miel
mee-ELL

**hood (n)**
la capucha
kah-POO-chah

**horn (n)**
el cuerno
koo'ER-no

**horrible (adj)**
horrible
o-RREE-bleh

**horse (n)**
el caballo
kah-BAH-yo

**horse riding (n)**
la equitación
eh-kee-tah-thi-ON

**hospital (n)**
el hospital
os-pee-TAHL

**hot (adj)**
caliente
kah-lee-EN-teh

**hot-air balloon (n)**
el globo aerostático
GLOH-bo
ah'eh-ro-STAH-tee-ko

**hot chocolate (n)**
el chocolate
caliente
cho-ko-LAH-teh
kah-lee-EN-teh

**hot dog (n)**
el perrito caliente
peh-RREE-to
kah-lee-EN-teh

**hotel (n)**
el hotel
o-TELL

**hour (n)**
la hora
O-rah

**house (n)**
la casa
KAH-sah

**how (adv)**
cómo
KO-mo

honey
la miel

**huge (adj)**
enorme
e-NOR-meh

**human (n)**
el humano
oo-MAH-no

**hummingbird (n)**
el colibrí
ko-lee-BREE

**hungry (adj)**
hambriento (m)
am-bree-EN-to

**hurricane (n)**
el huracán
oo-rah-KAHN

**husband (n)**
el marido
mah-REE-do

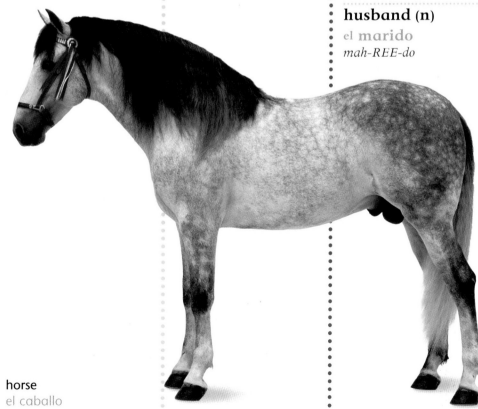

horse
el caballo

A B C D E F G H I J K L M N O P Q R S T U V W X Y Z

island
la isla

**I (pron)**
yo
*yo*

**ice (n)**
el hielo
*e-EH-lo*

**ice cream (n)**
el helado
*eh-LAH-do*

**ice cube (n)**
el cubito de hielo
*koo-BE-to deh e-EH-lo*

ice cream
el helado

**ice hockey (n)**
el hockey sobre hielo
*HO-kay SO-breh e-EH-lo*

**ice lolly (n)**
el polo
*PO-lo*

**ice skating (n)**
el patinaje sobre hielo
*pah-tee-NAH-Heh so-breh e-EH-lo*

**idea (n)**
la idea
*ee-DEE-ah*

**ill (adj)**
el enfermo (m)
*en-FAIR-mo*

**illness (n)**
la enfermedad
*en-fair-meh-DAHD*

**immediately (adv)**
inmediatamente
*in-meh-dee-ah-tah-MEN-teh*

**important (adj)**
importante
*im-por-TAN-teh*

**impossible (adj)**
imposible
*im-po-SEE-bleh*

**information (n)**
la información
*in-for-mah-thi-ON*

**ingredient (n)**
el ingrediente
*in-greh-dee-EN-teh*

**injury (n)**
la herida
*eh-REE-dah*

**ink (n)**
la tinta
*TEEN-tah*

**insect (n)**
el insecto
*in-SEK-to*

**inside (prep)**
dentro, dentro de
*DEN-tro/DEN-tro deh*

**instruction (n)**
la instrucción
*ins-trook-thi-ON*

**instrument (n)**
el instrumento
*ins-troo-MEN-to*

**interesting (adj)**
interesante
*in-teh-reh-SAN-teh*

**international (adj)**
internacional
*in-tair-nah-thi-o-NAHL*

**Internet (n)**
el Internet
*in-tair-NET*

**into (prep)**
en
*en*

**invitation (n)**
la invitación
*in-be-tah-thi-ON*

**iron (clothes) (n)**
la plancha
*PLAHN-cha*

**island (n)**
la isla
*ISS-lah*

**it (pron)**
la (f), lo (m)
*lah/lo*

**its (adj)**
su (sing), sus (plu)
*soo/soos*

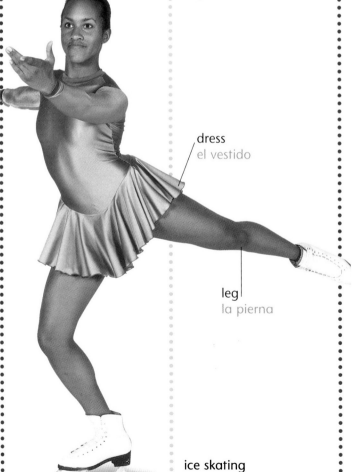

dress
el vestido

leg
la pierna

ice skating
el patinaje sobre hielo

# J

jug
la jarra

**jacket (n)**
la chaqueta
*chah-KEH-tah*

**jam (n)**
la mermelada
*mair-meh-LAH-dah*

**jeans (n)**
los vaqueros
*bah-KEH-ross*

**jellyfish (n)**
la medusa
*meh-DOO-sah*

**jet (n)**
el jet
*yet*

**jewel (n)**
la joya
*HO-yah*

**jewellery (n)**
las joyas
*HO-yahs*

**job (n)**
el trabajo
*trah-BAH-Ho*

**joke (n)**
la broma
*BRO-mah*

**journey (n)**
el viaje
*be-AH-Heh*

**judo (n)**
el judo
*HOO-do*

**jug (n)**
la jarra
*HAH-rrah*

**juice (n)**
el zumo
*THOO-mo*

**jumper (n)**
el jersey
*Her-SAY*

**jungle (n)**
la selva
*SEHL-bah*

**just (adv)**
justo
*HOOS-to*

jeans
los vaqueros

# K

kite
la cometa

**kangaroo (n)**
el canguro
*kan-GOO-ro*

**karate (n)**
el kárate
*KAH-rah-teh*

**kettle (n)**
el hervidor de agua
*air-be-DOR deh AH-goo'ah*

**key (n)**
la llave
*YAH-beh*

**keyboard (n)**
el teclado
*teh-KLAH-do*

**kind (gentle) (adj)**
amable
*ah-MAH-bleh*

**kind (type) (adj)**
tipo
*TEE-po*

**king (n)**
el rey
*rreh'e*

**kiss (n)**
el beso
*BEH-so*

**kitchen (n)**
la cocina
*ko-THI-nah*

**kite (n)**
la cometa
*ko-MEH-tah*

**kitten (n)**
el gatito
*gah-TEE-to*

**knee (n)**
la rodilla
*rro-DEE-yah*

**knife (n)**
el cuchillo
*koo-CHEE-yo*

**knight (n)**
el caballero
*kah-bah-YEH-ro*

**knot (n)**
el nudo
*NOO-do*

**koala (n)**
el koala
*ko-AH-lah*

kitten
el gatito

tail
la cola

A B C D E F G H I **J K** L M N O P Q R S T U V W X Y Z

# L

lemon
el limón

**ladder (n)**
la escalera
ess-KAH-leh-rah

**ladybird (n)**
la mariquita
mah-ree-KEE-tah

**lake (n)**
el lago
LAH-go

**lamb (n)**
el cordero
kor-DEH-roh

**lamp (n)**
la lámpara
LAHM-pah-rah

**land (n)**
la tierra
tee-AIR-rrah

**language (n)**
el idioma
la lengua
e-dee-O-mah/LEN-goo'ah

**laptop (n)**
el (ordenador)
portátil
(or-den-a-DOR)
por-TAH-til

**last (adj)**
último
OOL-tee-mo

**late (adv)**
tarde
TAR-deh

**lawn (n)**
el césped
THESS-ped

**lawn mower (n)**
el cortacésped
kor-tah-THESS-ped

**layer (n)**
la capa
KAH-pah

**lazy (adj)**
vago (m)
BAH-go

**leaf (n)**
la hoja
O-Hah

**leather (n)**
el cuero
koo'EH-ro

**left (adj)**
izquierda (f)
ith-kee-AIR-dah

**left-handed (adj)**
zurdo (m)
THOOR-do

**leg (n)**
la pierna
pee-AIR-nah

**lemon (n)**
el limón
lee-MON

**lemonade (n)**
la limonada
lee-mon-AH-dah

**leopard (n)**
el leopardo
leh-o-PAR-do

**lesson (n)**
la lección
lek-thi-ON

**letter (alphabet) (n)**
la letra
LEH-trah

**letter (postal) (n)**
la carta
KAR-tah

**letter box (n)**
el buzón
boo-THON

**lettuce (n)**
la lechuga
leh-CHOO-gah

**level (adj)**
nivelado (m)
nee-bell-AH-do

**library (n)**
la biblioteca
bib-lee-o-TEH kah

**lid (n)**
la tapa
TAH-pah

**life (n)**
la vida
BE-dah

**life jacket (n)**
el salvavidas
sahl-bah-BE-dahs

**lifeboat (n)**
el bote salvavidas
BO-teh sahl-bah-BE-dahs

**lifeguard (n)**
el/la socorrista (m/f)
so-kor-RREES-tah

**lift (n)**
el ascensor
ahs-then-SOR

**light (n)**
la luz
looth

**light (not
heavy) (adj)**
ligero (m)
lee-GEH-ro

**lighthouse (n)**
el faro
FAH-ro

**lightning (n)**
el relámpago
rreh-LAHM-pah-go

**like (prep)**
como
KO-mo

**line (n)**
la línea
LEE-neh-ah

**lion (n)**
el león
leh-ON

**lipstick (n)**
la barra de labios
BAH-rrah deh
LAH-be-oss

**list (n)**
la lista
LISS-tah

**little (adj)**
pequeño (m)
peh-KEH-n'yo

**living room (n)**
el salón
sah-LON

**lizard (n)**
la lagartija
lah-gar-TEE-Hah

lizard
la lagartija

# M

**lobster (n)**
la langosta
*lahn-GOSS-tah*

**location (n)**
la situación
*see-too-ah-thi-ON*

**long (adj)**
largo (m)
*LAR-go*

**loose (adj)**
flojo (m)
*FLO-Ho*

**lorry (n)**
el camión
*kah-mee-ON*

**(a) lot (adj)**
mucho (m)
*MOO-cho*

**loud (adj)**
alto (m)
*AHL-to*

**lovely (adj)**
precioso (m)
*preh-thi-O-so*

**low (adj)**
bajo (m)
*BAH-Ho*

**lucky (adj)**
afortunado (m)
*ah-for-too-NAH-do*

**luggage (n)**
el equipaje
*eh-kee-PAH-Heh*

**lunch (n)**
la comida
*ko-MEE-dah*

**lunch box (n)**
la fiambrera
*fee-am-BREH-rah*

**lunch break (n)**
la hora de la
comida
*O-rah deh lah
ko-MEE-dah*

tail
la cola

mask
la máscara

**machine (n)**
la máquina
*MAH-kee-nah*

**magazine (n)**
la revista
*reh-BISS-tah*

**magician (n)**
el mago
*MAH-go*

**magnet (n)**
el imán
*e-MAHN*

**magnetic (adj)**
magnético (m)
*mahg-NEH-tee-ko*

**magnifying
glass (n)**
la lupa
*LOO-pah*

**mail (n)**
el correo
*kor-RREH-o*

**main (adj)**
principal
*prin-thi-PAHL*

**make-up (n)**
el maquillaje
*mah-kee-YAH-Heh*

**male (adj)**
el varón
*bah-RON*

**mammal (n)**
el mamífero
*mah-MEE-feh-ro*

**man (n)**
el hombre
*OM-breh*

**many (adj)**
muchos
*MOO-chos*

**map (n)**
el mapa
*MAH-pah*

**marbles (toy) (n)**
las canicas
*kah-NEE-kahs*

**mark (n)**
la marca
*MAR-kah*

**market (n)**
el mercado
*mair-KAH-do*

**married (adj)**
casado (m)
*kah-SAH-do*

**mask (n)**
la máscara
*MAHS-kah-rah*

**mat (n)**
la esterilla
*ess-teh-REE-yah*

**match (sport) (n)**
el partido
*par-TEE-do*

**matchbox (n)**
la caja de cerillas
*KAH-Hah deh
theh-REE-yahs*

**maths (n)**
las matemáticas
*mah-teh-MAH-tee-kahs*

**maybe (adv)**
a lo mejor
*ah lo meh-HOR*

**me (pron)**
me
*meh*

**meal (n)**
la comida
*ko-MEE-dah*

**meaning (n)**
el significado
*sig-nee-fee-KAH-do*

**measurement (n)**
la medida
*meh-DEE-dah*

**meat (n)**
la carne
*KAR-neh*

**medicine (n)**
la medicina
*meh-dee-THI-nah*

**melon (n)**
el melón
*meh-LON*

**member (n)**
el miembro
*mee-EM-bro*

melon
el melón

A B C D E F G H I J K **L M** N O P Q R S T U V W X Y Z

75

milk shake
el batido

**menu (n)**
el menú
*meh-NOO*

**mess (n)**
el desorden
*deh-SOR-den*

**message (n)**
el mensaje
*men-SAH-Heh*

**metal (n)**
el metal
*meh-TAHL*

**microwave (n)**
el microondas
*mee-kro-ON-dahs*

**middle (n)**
el centro
*THEN-tro*

**midnight (n)**
la medianoche
*meh-dee-ah-NO-cheh*

**milk (n)**
la leche
*LEH-cheh*

**milk shake (n)**
el batido
*bah-TEE-do*

**million**
millón
*mee-YON*

**mineral (n)**
el mineral
*mee-neh-RAHL*

**minute (time) (n)**
el minuto
*mee-NOO-to*

**mirror (n)**
el espejo
*ess-PEH-Ho*

**mistake (n)**
el error
*air-RROR*

**mitten (n)**
la manopla
*mah-NO-plah*

**mixture (n)**
la mezcla
*METH-klah*

**mobile phone (n)**
el teléfono móvil
*teh-LEH-fo-no MO-beel*

**money (n)**
el dinero
*dee-NEH-ro*

**monkey (n)**
el mono
*MO-no*

**monster (n)**
el monstruo
*MONS-troo'o*

**month (n)**
el mes
*mess*

mitten
la manopla

**moon (n)**
la luna
*LOO-nah*

**more than**
más de (numbers)
más que
*mahs deh/mahs keh*

**morning (n)**
la mañana
*mah-N'YAH-nah*

**mosque (n)**
la mezquita
*meth-KEE-tah*

**most (adj)**
mayoría
*mah-yo-REE-ah*

**moth (n)**
la polilla
*po-LEE-yah*

**mother (n)**
la madre
*MAH-dreh*

**motor (n)**
el motor
*mo-TOR*

**motorbike (n)**
la motocicleta
*mo-to-thi-KLEH-tah*

**motorway (n)**
la autopista
*ah'oo-to-PISS-tah*

**mountain (n)**
la montaña
*mon-TAH-n'yah*

**mountain bike (n)**
la bicicleta de montaña
*be-thi-KLEH-tah de mon-TAH-n'yah*

**mouse (animal/ computer) (n)**
el ratón
*rrah-TON*

**mouse mat (n)**
la alfombrilla
*ahl-fom-BREE-yah*

**moustache (n)**
el bigote
*be-GO-teh*

**mouth (n)**
la boca
*BO-kah*

**mud (n)**
el barro
*BAR-rro*

**muddy (adj)**
embarrado (m)
*em-bar-RRAH-do*

**muesli (n)**
el muesli
*moo-EHS-lee*

**mug (n)**
la taza
*TAH-thah*

**mum (n)**
la mamá
*mah-MAH*

**museum (n)**
el museo
*moo-SEH-o*

**mushroom (n)**
el champiñón
*cham-pee-N'YON*

**music (n)**
la música
*MOO-see-kah*

**musician (n)**
el músico
*MOO-see-ko*

**my (adj)**
mi
*mee*

mushroom
el champiñón

# N

necklace
el collar

**nail (n)**
la uña
OO-n'yah

**name (n)**
el nombre
NOM-breh

**narrow (adj)**
estrecho (m)
ess-TREH-cho

**national (adj)**
nacional
nah-thi-o-NAHL

**nature (n)**
la naturaleza
nah-too-rah-LEH-thah

nest
el nido

**naughty (adj)**
travieso (m)
trah-be-EH-so

**near (adv)**
cerca
THAIR-kah

**nearly (adv)**
casi
KAH-see

**neck (n)**
el cuello
koo-EH-yo

**necklace (n)**
el collar
ko-YAR

**needle (n)**
la aguja
ah-GOO-Hah

**neighbour (n)**
el vecino
beh-THI-no

**neighbourhood (n)**
el vecindario
beh-theen-DAH-ree-o

**nephew (n)**
el sobrino
so-BREE-no

**nest (n)**
el nido
NEE-do

**net (n)**
la red
rred

**never (adv)**
nunca
NOON-kah

**new (adj)**
nuevo (m)
noo'EH-bo

**news (n)**
las noticias
no-TEE-thi-ahs

**newspaper (n)**
el periódico
peh-ree-O-dee-ko

**next (adj)**
próximo (m)
PROK-see-mo

**nice (adj)**
bueno
boo'EH-no

**niece (n)**
la sobrina
so-BREE-nah

**night (n)**
la noche
NO-cheh

**nobody (pron)**
nadie
NAH-dee-eh

**noisy (adj)**
ruidoso (m)
rroo'e-DO-so

**noodle (n)**
el fideo
fee-DEH-o

**north (n)**
el norte
NOR-teh

**nose (n)**
la nariz
nah-REETH

**note (n)**
la nota
NO-tah

**notebook (n)**
la libreta
lee-BREH-tah

noodles
los fideos

**nothing (pron)**
nada
NAH-dah

**now (adv)**
ahora
ah-O-rah

**nowhere (adv)**
ninguna parte
nin-GOO-nah PAR-teh

**number (n)**
el número
NOO-meh-ro

**nurse (n)**
la enfermera (f)
el enfermero (m)
en-fair-MEH-rah/ro

**nursery (n)**
la guardería
goo'ar-deh-REE-ah

felt-tip pen
el rotulador

notebook
la libreta

A B C D E F G H I J K L M **N** O P Q R S T U V W X Y Z

ocean
el océano

**oar (n)**
el remo
*RREH-mo*

**object (n)**
el objeto
*ob-HEH-to*

**ocean (n)**
el océano
*o-thi-AH-no*

**of (prep)**
de, del (de + el)
*deh/del*

**office (n)**
la oficina
*o-fee-THI-nah*

**often (adv)**
a menudo
*ah meh-NOO-do*

onion
la cebolla

**oil (n)**
el aceite
*ah-THEH-e-teh*

**old (adj)**
viejo (m)
*be-EH-Ho*

**old person (n)**
la persona mayor
*pair-SO-nah mah-YOR*

**Olympic Games (n)**
los Juegos
Olímpicos
*Hoo'EH-goss
oh-LIM-pee-koss*

**on top of (prep)**
encima de
*en-THI-mah deh*

**onion (n)**
la cebolla
*theh-BO-yah*

**only (adv)**
sólamente
*so-lah-MEN-teh*

**open (adj)**
abierto (m)
*ah-be-AIR-to*

**opening hours (n)**
las horas de
apertura
*O-rahs deh
ah-pair-TOO-rah*

orange
la naranja

orange juice
el zumo de naranja

**operation (n)**
la operación
*o-pair-ah-thi-ON*

**opposite (prep)**
enfrente de
*en-FREN-teh deh*

**opposites (adj)**
contrarios (m)
*kon-TRAH-ree-os*

**or (conj)**
o
*o*

**orange (colour) (adj)**
naranja
*nah-RAHN-Hah*

**orange (fruit) (n)**
la naranja
*nah-RAHN-Hah*

**orange juice (n)**
el zumo de
naranja
*THOO-mo deh
nah-RAHN-Hah*

**orchestra (n)**
la orquesta
*or-KESS-tah*

**other (adj)**
otro (m)
*O-tro*

**ouch!**
¡ay!
*ay*

**our (adj)**
nuestra (f)
nuestro (m)
nuestras (f plu)
nuestros (m plu)
*noo'ESS-trah/tro/trahs/
tros*

**out of (prep)**
fuera de
*foo'EH-rah deh*

**outside (adv)**
afuera
*ah-foo'EH-rah*

**oval (n)**
el óvalo
*O-bah-lo*

**oven (n)**
el horno
*OR-no*

**oven glove (n)**
el guante del
horno
*goo'AHN-teh dell OR-no*

**over there (adv)**
ahí
*ah-E*

**owl (n)**
el búho
*BOO-o*

**own (adj)**
propio (m)
*PRO-pee-o*

owl
el búho

# P

pear
la pera

paint tin
el bote de pintura

**page (n)**
la página
*PAH-He-nah*

**paint (n)**
la pintura
*pin-TOO-rah*

**paint tin (n)**
el bote de pintura
*BO-teh deh pin-TOO-rah*

**paintbrush (n)**
el pincel
*pin-THELL*

**painting (n)**
el cuadro
la pintura
*koo'AH-dro/pin-TOO-rah*

**pair (n)**
el par
*par*

**palm tree (n)**
la palmera
*pahl-MEH-rah*

**pancake (n)**
el crepe
*KREH-peh*

**panda (n)**
el panda
*PAN-dah*

**paper (n)**
el papel
*pah-PEL*

**paper clip (n)**
el clip
*KLEEP*

**paper towel (n)**
la servilleta
de papel
*ser-bee-YEH-tah deh pah-PEL*

**parade (n)**
el desfile
*dess-FEE-leh*

**parasol (n)**
la sombrilla
*som-BREE-yah*

**parents (n)**
los padres
*PAH-drehs*

**park (n)**
el parque
*PAR-keh*

**parrot (n)**
el loro
*LO-ro*

**part (n)**
la parte
*PAR-teh*

**partner (n)**
la compañera (f)
el compañero (m)
*kom-pah-N'YEH-rah/ro*

**party (n)**
la fiesta
*fee-ESS-tah*

**passenger (n)**
la pasajera (f)
el pasajero (m)
*pah-sah-HEH-rah/ro*

**passport (n)**
el pasaporte
*pah-sah-POR-teh*

**past (history) (n)**
el pasado
*pah-SAH-do*

**past (prep)**
por delante de
*por deh-LAHN-teh deh*

**pasta (n)**
la pasta
*PAHS-tah*

**path (n)**
el camino
*kah-MEE-no*

**patient (n)**
el/la paciente (m/f)
*pah-thi-EN-teh*

**patient (adj)**
paciente
*pah-thi-EN-teh*

**pattern (n)**
el diseño
*dee-SEH-n'yo*

**pavement (n)**
la acera
*ah-THEH-rah*

**paw (n)**
la pata
*PAH-tah*

**pay (n)**
el sueldo
*soo'ELL-do*

**pea (n)**
el guisante
*ghee-SAHN-teh*

**peace (n)**
la paz
*pa'ath*

**peaceful (adj)**
tranquilo (m)
*trahn-KEE-lo*

**peanut (n)**
el cacahuete
*kah-kah-oo'EH-teh*

**pear (n)**
la pera
*PEH-rah*

**pebble (n)**
la piedra
*pee-EH-drah*

**pedal (n)**
el pedal
*peh-DAHL*

**pelican (n)**
el pelícano
*peh-LEE-kah-no*

pelican • el pelícano

wing
el ala

beak
el pico

pelican
el pelícano

A B C D E F G H I J K L M N O **P** Q R S T U V W X Y Z

79

**pen (n)**
el bolígrafo
*bo-LEE-grah-fo*

**pencil (n)**
el lápiz
*LAH-pith*

**pencil case (n)**
el estuche
*ess-TOO-cheh*

**penguin (n)**
el pingüino
*pin-goo'E-no*

**people (n)**
la gente
*HEN-teh*

**pepper (n)**
la pimienta
*pee-mee'EN-tah*

**perfect (adj)**
perfecto (m)
*pair-FEK-to*

**perhaps (adv)**
quizás
*kee-THAHS*

**person (n)**
la persona
*pair-SO-nah*

piano
el piano

**pet (n)**
el animal de compañía
*ah-nee-MAHL deh kom-pah-N'YEE-ah*

**petrol (n)**
la gasolina
*gah-so-LEE-nah*

**phone (n)**
el teléfono
*teh-LEH-fo-no*

**photo (n)**
la foto
*FO-to*

**phrase (n)**
la frase
*FRAH-seh*

**piano (n)**
el piano
*pee-AH-no*

**picnic (n)**
el picnic
*PEEK-neek*

pinecone
la piña

**picture (n)**
el cuadro
*koo'AH-dro*

**piece (n)**
el trozo
*TRO-tho*

**pig (n)**
el cerdo
*THAIR-do*

**pillow (n)**
la almohada
*ahl-mo-AH-dah*

**pilot (n)**
el/la piloto (m/f)
*pee-LO-to*

**pine tree (n)**
el pino
*PEE-no*

**pineapple (n)**
la piña
*PEE-n'yah*

**pinecone (n)**
la piña
*PEE-n'yah*

**pink (adj)**
rosa
*RRO-sah*

**pizza (n)**
la pizza
*PEE-thah*

**plane (n)**
el avión
*ah-be-ON*

**planet (n)**
el planeta
*plah-NEH-tah*

**plant (n)**
la planta
*PLAHN-tah*

**plastic (adj)**
plástico (m)
*PLAHS-tee-ko*

**plate (n)**
el plato
*PLAH-to*

**platform (n)**
el andén
*ahn-DEN*

**play (n)**
la obra
*O-brah*

**player (n)**
el jugador (m)
la jugadora (f)
*Hoo-gah-DOR/ah*

**playground (n)**
el patio de recreo
*PAH-tee-oh deh rreh-KREH-o*

pine tree
el pino

**playtime (n)**
la hora del recreo
*O-rah del rreh-KREH-o*

**please (adv)**
por favor
*por fah-BOR*

**plug (sink) (n)**
el tapón
*tah-PON*

**pocket (n)**
el bolsillo
*bol-SEE-yo*

**pocket money (n)**
el dinero de bolsillo
*dee-NEH-ro deh*
*bol-SEE-yo*

**polar bear (n)**
el oso polar
*O-so po-LAR*

**police (n)**
la policía
*po-lee-THI-ah*

**police car (n)**
el coche de la
policía
*KO-cheh deh lah*
*po-lee-THI-ah*

**police
helicopter (n)**
el helicóptero de
la policía
*eh-lee-KOP-teh-ro deh*
*lah po-lee-THI-ah*

**pond (n)**
el estanque
*ess-TAN-keh*

**poor (adj)**
pobre
*PO-breh*

**popular (adj)**
tener éxito
*teh-NAIR EKS-e-to*

**possible (adj)**
posible
*po-SEE-bleh*

**post office (n)**
la oficina de
correos
*o-fee-THI-nah deh*
*ko-RREH-oss*

**postbox (n)**
el buzón
*boo-THON*

**postcard (n)**
la postal
*pos-TAHL*

**postcode (n)**
el código postal
*KO-dee-go pos-TAHL*

**poster (n)**
el póster
*POS-tair*

**postman (n)**
el cartero
*kah-TEH-ro*

**potato (n)**
la patata
*pah-TAH-tah*

**pouch (animal) (n)**
la bolsa
*BOL-sah*

**powder (n)**
el polvo
*POL-bo*

**present (n)**
el regalo
*rreh-GAH-lo*

**president (n)**
la presidenta (f)
el presidente (m)
*preh-see-DEN-tah/teh*

**pretty (adj)**
bonito (m)
*bo-NEE-to*

**price (n)**
el precio
*PREH-thi-o*

puppet
la marioneta

**prime minister (n)**
la primer
ministra (f)
el primer
ministro (m)
*pre-MAIR*
*mee-NISS-trah/tro*

**prince (n)**
el príncipe
*PRIN-thi-peh*

**princess (n)**
la princesa
*prin-THEH-sah*

**prize (n)**
el premio
*PREH-mee-o*

**probably (adv)**
probablemente
*pro-bah-bleh-MEN-teh*

**problem (n)**
el problema
*pro-BLEH-mah*

**programme (n)**
el programa
*pro-GRAH-mah*

**project (n)**
el proyecto
*pro-YEK-to*

**pudding (n)**
el pudín
*poo-DIN*

**pumpkin (n)**
la calabaza
*kah-lah-BAH-thah*

**pupil (n)**
la alumna (f)
el alumno (m)
*ah-LOOM-nah/no*

**puppet (n)**
la marioneta
*mah-ree-o-NEH-tah*

**puppet show (n)**
el teatro de
marionetas
*tee-AH-tro deh*
*mah-ree-o-NEH-tahs*

**puppy (n)**
el cachorro
*kah-CHOR-rro*

**purple (adj)**
púrpura
*POOR-poo-rah*

**purse (n)**
el monedero
*mo-neh-DEH-ro*

**puzzle (n)**
el rompecabezas
*rrom-peh-kah-BEH-thahs*

**pyjamas (n)**
el pijama
*pee-HAH-mah*

purse
el monedero

A
B
C
D
E
F
G
H
I
J
K
L
M
N
O
**P**
Q
R
S
T
U
V
W
X
Y
Z

A B C D E F G H I J K L M N O P **Q R** S T U V W X Y Z

# Q R

## quarter (n)
el **cuarto**
*koo´AR-to*

## queen (n)
la **reina**
*RREH´e-nah*

## question (n)
la **pregunta**
*preh-GOON-tah*

## queue (n)
la **cola**
*KO-lah*

## quickly (adv)
**rápidamente**
*rrah-pee-dah-MEN-teh*

## quiet (adj)
**tranquilo** (m)
*trahn-KEE-lo*

## quietly (adv)
**tranquilamente**
*trahn-kee-lah-MEN-teh*

## quiz (n)
el **concurso**
*kon-KOOR-so*

queen
la **reina**

racing car
el coche de carreras

## rabbit (n)
el **conejo**
*ko-NEH-Ho*

## race (n)
la **carrera**
*kar-RREH-rah*

## racing car (n)
el **coche de carreras**
*KO-cheh deh kar-RREH-rahs*

## racket (n)
la **raqueta**
*rrah-KEH-tah*

## radio (n)
la **radio**
*RRAH-dee-o*

## railway station (n)
la **estación de tren**
*ess-tah-thi-ON deh tren*

## rain (n)
la **lluvia**
*YOO-be-ah*

## rainbow (n)
el **arco iris**
*AR-ko EE-riss*

## raincoat (n)
el **impermeable**
*im-pair-meh-AH-bleh*

## rainforest (n)
la **selva tropical**
*SEL-bah tro-pee-KAHL*

## rake (n)
el **rastrillo**
*rrahs-TREE-yo*

## raspberry (n)
la **frambuesa**
*fram-boo'EH-sah*

## rat (n)
la **rata**
*RAH-tah*

## reading (n)
la **lectura**
*lek-TOO-rah*

## ready (adj)
**listo**
*LISS-to*

## real (adj)
**verdadero** (m)
*bair-dah-DEH-ro*

## really (adv)
**de verdad**
*deh bair-DAHD*

## receipt (n)
el **recibo**
*rreh-THI-bo*

## recipe (n)
la **receta**
*rreh-THEH-tah*

## rectangle (n)
el **rectángulo**
*rrek-TAN-goo-lo*

## red (adj)
**rojo** (m)
*RRO-Ho*

## reef (n)
el **arrecife**
*ar-rreh-THI-feh*

## reindeer (n)
el **reno**
*RREH-no*

## remote control (n)
el **mando a distancia**
*MAAN-doh ah dees-TAN-thiah*

## report (n)
el **informe**
*in-FOR-meh*

## rescue (n)
el **rescate**
*rress-KAH-teh*

## restaurant (n)
el **restaurante**
*rress-tah'oo-RAHN-teh*

## rhinoceros (n)
el **rinoceronte**
*ree-no-theh-RON-teh*

## ribbon (n)
el **lazo**
*LAH-tho*

## rice (n)
el **arroz**
*ar-RROTH*

## rich (adj)
**rico** (m)
*RREE-ko*

## riding (n)
la **equitación**
*eh-kee-tah-thi-ON*

## right (correct) (adj)
**correcto** (m)
*kor-RREK-to*

**right (not left) (adj)**
la derecha (f)
deh-REH-chah

**ring (n)**
el anillo
ah-NEE-yo

**ripe (adj)**
maduro (m)
mah-DOO-ro

**river (n)**
el río
RREE-o

**road (n)**
la calle
KAH-yeh

**robot (n)**
el robot
rro-BOT

**rock (n)**
la roca
RRO-kah

**rocket (n)**
el cohete
ko-EH-teh

**roller skating (n)**
el patinaje
sobre ruedas
pah-tee-NAH-Heh
SOH-breh roo-EH-dahs

**rollerblading (n)**
el patinaje en línea
pah-tee-NAH-Heh
en LEE-nee-ah

**roof (n)**
el tejado
teh-HAH-do

**room (n)**
la habitación
ah-be-tah-thi-ON

**root (n)**
la raíz
rrah'EETH

**rope (n)**
la cuerda
koo'AIR-dah

**rose (n)**
la rosa
RRO-sah

**rough (adj)**
áspero (m)
AHS-peh-ro

**round (adj)**
redondo (m)
rre-DON-do

**roundabout (n)**
el carrusel
kar-rroo-SEL

**route (n)**
la ruta
RROO-tah

**rowing (n)**
el remo
RREH-mo

**rowing boat (n)**
el bote de remos
BO-teh deh RREH-mos

**rubber (eraser) (n)**
la goma de borrar
GO-mah deh bor-RRAR

**rubber band (n)**
la goma
GO-mah

**rubbish (n)**
la basura
bah-SOO-rah

**rucksack (n)**
la mochila
mo-CHEE-lah

**rug (n)**
la alfombra
ahl-FOM-brah

**rugby (n)**
el rugby
RROOG-be

**ruler
(measuring) (n)**
la regla
RREG-lah

saddle
la silla de
montar

**sack (n)**
el saco
SAH-ko

**sad (adj)**
triste
TRISS-teh

**saddle (bike) (n)**
el sillín
see-YEEN

**saddle (horse) (n)**
la silla de montar
SEE-yah deh mon-TAR

**safe (adj)**
seguro (m)
seh-GOO-ro

**sail (n)**
la vela
BEH-lah

**sailing (n)**
la vela
BEH-lah

**sailing boat (n)**
el barco de vela
BAR-ko deh BE-lah

**sailor (n)**
el marinero
mah-ree-NEH-ro

**salad (n)**
la ensalada
en-sah-LAH-dah

**salt (n)**
la sal
sahl

**same (adj)**
lo mismo (m)
MEES-mo

**sand (n)**
la arena
ah-REH-nah

**sandal (n)**
la sandalia
san-DAH-lee-ah

**sandcastle (n)**
el castillo de arena
kahs-TEE-yo deh
ah-REH-nah

**sandwich (n)**
el sándwich
SAND-weech

**saucepan (n)**
la olla
O-yah

**scarf (n)**
la bufanda
boo-FAN-dah

**school (n)**
la escuela
ess-koo'EH-lah

**school bag (n)**
la cartera
del colegio
kar-TEH-rah
del ko-LEH-Hee-o

**school uniform (n)**
el uniforme escolar
oo-nee-FOR-meh
ess-ko-LAR

scarf
la bufanda

S

scissors
las tijeras

**science (n)**
la ciencia
*thi-EN-thi-ah*

**scientist (n)**
la científica (f)
el científico (m)
*thi-en-TEE-fee-kah/ko*

**scissors (n)**
las tijeras
*tee-HEH-rahs*

**score (n)**
el resultado
*reh-sool-TAH-do*

**screen (n)**
la pantalla
*pan-TAH-yah*

**sea (n)**
el mar
*mar*

**sea lion (n)**
el león marino
*leh-ON mah-REE-no*

**seafood (n)**
el marisco
*mah-REES-ko*

**seagull (n)**
la gaviota
*gah-be-O-tah*

**seal (n)**
la foca
*FO-kah*

**seaside (n)**
la costa
*KOSS-tah*

**season (n)**
la estación
*ess-tah-thi-ON*

**seaweed (n)**
el alga
*AHL-gah*

**second (2nd) (adj)**
segundo (m)
*seh-GOON-do*

**seed (n)**
la semilla
*seh-MEE-yah*

**semicircle (n)**
el semicírculo
*seh-mee-THEER-koo-lo*

**sense (n)**
el sentido
*sen-TEE-do*

**shadow (n)**
la sombra
*SOM-brah*

**shallow (adj)**
poco profundo (m)
*PO-ko pro-FOON-do*

**shampoo (n)**
el champú
*cham-POO*

**shape (n)**
la forma
*FOR-mah*

**shark (n)**
el tiburón
*tee-boo-RON*

**sharp (adj)**
afilado (m)
*ah-fee-LAH-do*

**she (pron)**
ella
*EH-yah*

**sheep (n)**
la oveja
*o-BEH-Hah*

**sheepdog (n)**
el perro pastor
*PEH-rroh pahs-TOR*

**sheet (bed) (n)**
la sábana
*SAH-bah-nah*

**shelf (n)**
el estante
*ess-TAN-teh*

**shell (n)**
la concha
*KON-chah*

**shiny (adj)**
brillante
*bree-YAN-teh*

**ship (n)**
el barco
*BAR-ko*

**shirt (n)**
la camisa
*kah-MEE-sah*

**shoe (n)**
el zapato
*thah-PAH-to*

**shop (n)**
la tienda
*tee-EN-dah*

**shop assistant (n)**
la dependienta (f)
el dependiente (m)
*deh-pen-dee-EN-tah/teh*

**shopper (n)**
el comprador (m)
la compradora (f)
*kom-prah-DOR/ah*

**shopping bag (n)**
la bolsa de la compra
*BOHL-sah deh la KOM-prah*

**shopping list (n)**
la lista de la compra
*LISS-tah deh la KOM-prah*

**shore (n)**
la orilla
*o-REE-yah*

**short (not tall) (adj)**
bajo (m)
*BAH-Ho*

**shorts (n)**
los pantalones cortos
*pan-tah-LO-nes KOR-tos*

**shoulder (n)**
el hombro
*OM-bro*

**show (n)**
el espectáculo
*ess-pek-TAH-koo-lo*

**shower (n)**
la ducha
*DOO-chah*

**shy (adj)**
tímido (m)
*TEE-mee-do*

**sick (adj)**
enfermo (m)
*en-FAIR-mo*

wool
la lana

sheep
las ovejas

**skating**
el patinaje

**helmet**
el casco

**T-shirt**
la camiseta

**shorts**
los pantalones
cortos

**sign (n)**
la señal
*seh-N'YAHL*

**silver (n)**
la plata
*PLAH-tah*

**simple (adj)**
sencillo (m)
*sen-THI-yo*

**sink (bathroom) (n)**
el lavabo
*lah-BAH-bo*

**sink (kitchen) (n)**
el fregadero
*freh-gah-DEH-ro*

**sister (n)**
la hermana
*air-MAH-nah*

**size (n)**
la talla
*TAH-yah*

**skateboard (n)**
el monopatín
*mo-no-pah-TEEN*

**skating (n)**
el patinaje
*pah-tee-NAH-Heh*

**skeleton (n)**
el esqueleto
*ess-keh-LEH-to*

**ski (n)**
el esquí
*ess-KEE*

**skiing (n)**
el esquí
*ess-KEE*

**skin (n)**
la piel
*pee-ELL*

**skipping rope (n)**
la cuerda
*koo'AIR-dah*

**skirt (n)**
la falda
*FAHL-dah*

**sky (n)**
el cielo
*thi-EH-lo*

**skyscraper (n)**
el rascacielos
*rahs-kah-thi-EH-los*

**sledge (n)**
el trineo
*tree-NEH-o*

**sleeping bag (n)**
el saco de dormir
*SAH-ko deh dor-MEER*

**sleeve (n)**
la manga
*MAHN-gah*

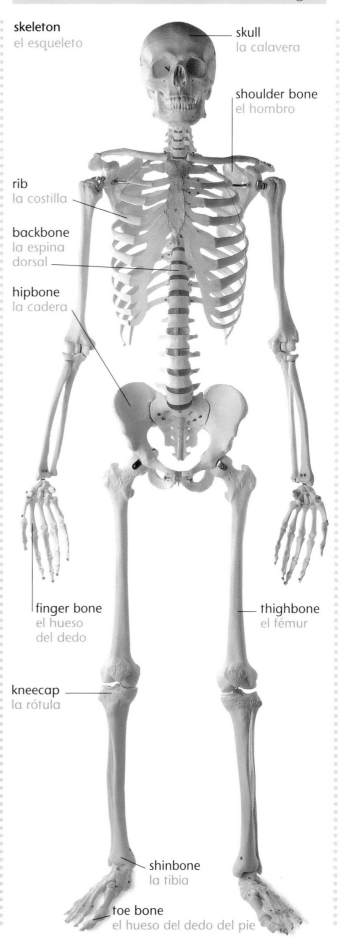

**skeleton**
el esqueleto

**skull**
la calavera

**shoulder bone**
el hombro

**rib**
la costilla

**backbone**
la espina
dorsal

**hipbone**
la cadera

**finger bone**
el hueso
del dedo

**thighbone**
el fémur

**kneecap**
la rótula

**shinbone**
la tibia

**toe bone**
el hueso del dedo del pie

A
B
C
D
E
F
G
H
I
J
K
L
M
N
O
P
Q
R
**S**
T
U
V
W
X
Y
Z

85

A B C D E F G H I J K L M N O P Q R **S** T U V W X Y Z

snake
la serpiente

tail
la cola

head
la cabeza

**sleigh (n)**
el trineo
tree-NEH-o

**slippers (n)**
las zapatillas
thah-pah-TEE-yahs

**slow (adj)**
lento (m)
LEN-to

**slowly (adv)**
despacio,
lentamente
des-PAH-thi-o/
len-tah-MEN-teh

**small (adj)**
pequeño (m)
peh-KEH-n'yo

**smell (n)**
el olor
o-LOR

**smoke (n)**
el humo
OO-mo

**smooth (adj)**
suave
soo'AH-beh

**snail (n)**
el caracol
kah-rah-KOL

**snake (n)**
la serpiente
ser-pee-EN-teh

**snorkelling (n)**
el buceo con tubo
boo-THEH-o kon
TOO-bo

**snow (n)**
la nieve
nee-EH-beh

**snowball (n)**
la bola de nieve
BO-lah deh nee-EH-beh

**snowboard (n)**
el snowboard
ess-NO-bord

**snowflake (n)**
el copo de nieve
KO-po deh nee-EH-beh

**snowman (n)**
el muñeco de nieve
moo-N'YEH-ko deh
nee-EH-beh

**snowmobile (n)**
la motonieve
mo-to-nee-EH-beh

**soap (n)**
el jabón
Hah-BON

**sock (n)**
el calcetín
kal-theh-TEEN

**sofa (n)**
el sofá
so-FAH

**soft (not hard) (adj)**
blando (m)
BLAHN-do

**soil (n)**
la tierra
tee-EH-rrah

**solid (n)**
sólido
SO-lee-do

**some (adj)**
alguna (f)
alguno (m)
algunas (f plu)
algunos (m plu)
ahl-GOON-ah/o/ahs/os

**some (article)**
unos
OO-nos

**someone (pron)**
alguien
AHLG-ee-en

**something (pron)**
algo
ahl-go

**sometimes (adv)**
algunas veces
ahl-GOO-nahs BEH-thess

**soon (adv)**
pronto
PRON-to

**south (n)**
el sur
soor

**souvenir (n)**
el regalo
rreh-GAH-lo

**space (n)**
el espacio
ess-PAH-thi-o

**space rocket (n)**
el cohete espacial
ko-EH-teh
ess-pah-thi'AHL

**spade (n)**
la pala
PAH-lah

**spaghetti (n)**
el spaghetti
ess-pah-GEH-tee

**Spanish (n)**
el español
ess-pah-N'YOL

**special (adj)**
especial
ess-PEH-thi-ahl

**speech (n)**
el discurso
diss-KOOR-so

**spider (n)**
la araña
ah-RAH-n'yah

**sponge (n)**
la esponja
ess-PON-Hah

**spoon (n)**
la cuchara
koo-CHAH-rah

shell
la concha

snail
el caracol

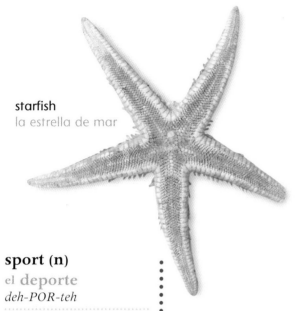
starfish
la estrella de mar

**sport (n)**
el deporte
*deh-POR-teh*

**spring (season) (n)**
la primavera
*pree-mah-BEH-rah*

**square (n)**
el cuadrado
*koo'ah-DRAH-do*

**squirrel (n)**
la ardilla
*ar-DEE-yah*

**stairs (n)**
la escalera
*ess-kah-LEH-rahs*

**stamp (n)**
el sello
*SEH-yo*

**star (n)**
la estrella
*ess-TREH-yah*

**starfish (n)**
la estrella de mar
*ess-TREH-yah deh mar*

**station (n)**
la estación
*ess-tah-thi-ON*

**steam (n)**
el vapor
*bah-POR*

**step (n)**
el paso
*PAH-so*

**stepfather (n)**
el padrastro
*pah-DRAHS-tro*

**stepmother (n)**
la madrastra
*mah-DRAHS-trah*

**stick (n)**
el palo
*PAH-lo*

**sticker (n)**
la pegatina
*peh-gah-TEE-nah*

**sticky (adj)**
pegajoso (m)
*peh-gah-HO-so*

**still (adj)**
quieto (m)
*kee-EH-to*

**still (adv)**
todavía
*to-dah-BEE-ah*

**stocking (n)**
la media
*MEH-dee-ah*

**stomach (n)**
el estómago
*ess-TO-mah-go*

**stone (n)**
la piedra
*pee-EH-drah*

**stormy (adj)**
tormentoso (m)
*tor-men-TO-so*

**story (n)**
la historia
*iss-TO-ree-ah*

**straight (adj)**
recto (m)
*RREK-to*

**strange (adj)**
raro (m)
*RRAH-ro*

**straw (n)**
la pajita
*pah-HE-tah*

**strawberry (n)**
la fresa
*FREH-sah*

**street (n)**
la calle
*KAH-yeh*

**street light (n)**
la farola
*fah-RO-lah*

**strict (adj)**
estricto (m)
*ess-TREEK-to*

**string (n)**
la cuerda
*koo'AIR-dah*

**stripes (n)**
las rayas
*RRAH-yahs*

**strong (adj)**
fuerte
*foo'AIR-teh*

strawberry
la fresa

**student (n)**
el/la estudiante (m/f)
*ess-too-dee-AN-teh*

**stupid (adj)**
estúpido (m)
*ess-TOO-pee-do*

**subject (n)**
el tema
*TEH-mah*

**submarine (n)**
el submarino
*soob-mah-REE-no*

**suddenly (adv)**
de repente
*deh-rreh-PEN-teh*

**sugar (n)**
el azúcar
*ah-THOO-kar*

**suit (n)**
el traje
*TRAH-Heh*

**suitcase (n)**
la maleta
*mah-LEH-tah*

**summer (n)**
el verano
*beh-RAH-no*

**sun (n)**
el sol
*sol*

**suncream (n)**
la crema solar
*KREH-mah so-LAR*

**sunflower (n)**
el girasol
*He-rah-SOL*

sunflower
el girasol

sunglasses • las gafas de sol

**sunglasses (n)**
las gafas de sol
*GAH-fahs deh sol*

**sunhat (n)**
la pamela
*pah-MEH-lah*

**sunlight (n)**
la luz solar
*looth so-LAR*

**sunny (adj)**
soleado (m)
*so-lee-AH-do*

**sunset (n)**
la puesta de sol
*poo'ESS-tah deh sol*

**supermarket (n)**
el supermercado
*soo-pair-mair-KAH-do*

**sure (adj)**
seguro (m)
*seh-GOO-ro*

**surface (n)**
la superficie
*soo-pair-FEE-thi-eh*

**surfboard (n)**
la tabla de surf
*TAH-blah de soorf*

swing
el columpio

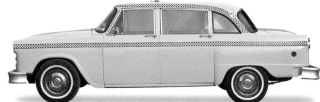

**surfing (n)**
el surf
*soorf*

**surgery (doctor's) (n)**
la consulta
*kon-SOOL-tah*

**surprise (n)**
la sorpresa
*sor-PREH-sah*

**surprising (adj)**
sorprendente
*sor-pren-DEN-teh*

**swan (n)**
el cisne
*THISS-neh*

**sweater (n)**
el jersey
*Her-SEY*

**sweet (n)**
el dulce
*DOOL-theh*

**swimming (n)**
la natación
*nah-tah-thi-ON*

**swimming pool (n)**
la piscina
*piss-THI-nah*

**swimsuit (n)**
el bañador
*bah-n'yah-DOR*

**swing (n)**
el columpio
*koh-LOOM-pee-o*

**symbol (n)**
el símbolo
*SEEM-bo-lo*

# T

tadpole
el renacuajo

**table (n)**
la mesa
*MEH-sah*

**table tennis (n)**
el tenis de mesa
*TEH-nees deh MEH-sah*

**tadpole (n)**
el renacuajo
*rreh-nah-koo'AH-Ho*

**tail (n)**
la cola
*KO-lah*

**tall (adj)**
alto (m)
*AHL-to*

**tap (n)**
el grifo
*GREE-fo*

**tape measure (n)**
la cinta métrica
*THEEN-tah MEH-tree-kah*

**taxi (n)**
el taxi
*TAK-see*

**tea (n)**
el té
*teh*

**tea towel (n)**
el paño de cocina
*PAH-n'yo de ko-THI-nah*

**teacher (n)**
el profesor (m)
la profesora (f)
*pro-feh-SOR/ah*

**team (n)**
el equipo
*eh-KEE-po*

**teddy bear (n)**
el osito de peluche
*o-SEE-to deh peh-LOO-cheh*

**telescope (n)**
el telescopio
*teh-less-KO-pee-o*

**television (n)**
la televisión
*teh-leh-be-see-ON*

**tennis (n)**
el tenis
*TEH-nees*

**tent (n)**
la tienda
*tee-EN-dah*

**term (n)**
el trimestre
*tree-MESS-treh*

**terrible (adj)**
terrible
*ter-RREE-bleh*

**text message (n)**
el mensaje de texto
*men-SAH-Heh deh TEKS-to*

taxi
el taxi

88

**that one (pron)**
aquél (m)
aquélla (f)
*ah-KEL/ah-KEH-ya*

**the (article)**
el (m)
la (f)
las (f plu)
los (m plu)
*ell/lah/lahs/loss*

**their (adj)**
su (sing), sus (plu)
*soo/soos*

**then (conj)**
entonces
*en-TON-thess*

**there (adv)**
allá, allí
*ah-YAH/ah-YEE*

**thermometer (n)**
el termómetro
*tair-MO-meh-tro*

**they (pron)**
ellas (f), ellos (m/f)
*EH-yahs/EH-yoss*

**thick (adj)**
grueso (m)
*groo'EH-so*

**thin (adj)**
delgado (m)
*del-GAH-do*

**thing (n)**
la cosa
*KO-sah*

**third (adj)**
tercero (m)
*tair-THAIR-o*

**thirsty (adj)**
sediento (m)
*seh-dee-EN-to*

**this (adj)**
esta (f), este (m)
*ESS-tah/teh*

**thousand**
mil
*meel*

**through (prep)**
por
*por*

**thumb (n)**
el pulgar
*pool-GAR*

**thunderstorm (n)**
la tormenta de
truenos
*tor-MEN-tah deh
troo'EH-nos*

**tick (n)**
la cruz
*krooth*

**ticket (n)**
el billete
*be-YEH-teh*

**tide (n)**
la marea
*mah-REH-ah*

**tie (n)**
la corbata
*kor-BAH-tah*

**tiger (n)**
el tigre
*TEE-greh*

**tight (adj)**
ajustado (m)
*ah-Hoos-TAH-do*

**till (cash
register) (n)**
la caja
*KAH-Hah*

toad
el sapo

tongue
la lengua

**time (What time
is it?) (n)**
la hora
*O-ra*

**time (I don't
have time.) (n)**
el tiempo
*tee-EM-po*

**timetable (n)**
el horario
*o-RAH-ree-o*

**tiny (adj)**
diminuto (m)
*dee-mee-NOO-to*

**tired (adj)**
cansado (m)
*kan-SAH-do*

**tissues (n)**
los pañuelos
de papel
*pah-n'yoo-EH-loss
deh pah-PEL*

**to (prep)**
a, al (a + el)
*ah/ahl*

**toad (n)**
el sapo
*SAH-po*

**toaster (n)**
el tostador
*toss-tah-DOR*

**today (adv)**
hoy
*oy*

**toe (n)**
el dedo del pie
*DEH-do del PEE'EH*

stripes
las rayas

tail
la cola

tiger
el tigre

A B C D E F G H I J K L M N O P Q R S **T** U V W X Y Z

89

toothbrush
el cepillo de dientes

**together (adv)**
juntos
HOON-toss

**toilet (n)**
el inodoro
ee-no-DOO-ro

**toilet (room) (n)**
el baño
BAH-n'yo

**toilet paper (n)**
el papel higiénico
pah-PEL ee-He-EN-ee-ko

**tomato (n)**
el tomate
to-MAH-teh

**tomorrow (adv)**
mañana
mah-N'YAH-nah

**tongue (n)**
la lengua
LEN-goo'ah

**tonight (adv)**
esta noche
ESS-tah NO-cheh

**too (adv)**
demasiado
deh-mah-see-AH-do

**tool (n)**
la herramienta
air-rrah-mee'EN-tah

tortoise
la tortuga

**tooth (n)**
el diente
dee-EN-teh

**toothbrush (n)**
el cepillo de dientes
theh-PEE-yo deh
dee-EN-tess

**toothpaste (n)**
la pasta de dientes
PAHS-tah deh
dee-EN-tess

**top (not bottom) (n)**
la cumbre
KOOM-breh

**torch (n)**
la linterna
lin-TAIR-nah

**tortoise (n)**
la tortuga
tor-TOO-gah

**toucan (n)**
el tucán
too-KAN

**tourist (n)**
el/la turista (m/f)
toor-ISS-tah

**towards (prep)**
hacia
AH-thi-ah

**towel (n)**
la toalla
to'AH-yah

**town (n)**
el pueblo
poo'EH-bloh

**toy (n)**
el juguete
Hoo-GEH-teh

**toy car (n)**
el coche de juguete
KO-cheh deh
Hoo-GEH-teh

**tractor (n)**
el tractor
trak-TOR

traffic lights
el semáforo

**traffic (n)**
el tráfico
TRAH-fee-ko

**traffic lights (n)**
el semáforo
seh-MAH-for-rro

**train (n)**
el tren
tren

**train set (n)**
el tren de juguete
tren deh Hoo-GEH-teh

**trainers (n)**
las zapatillas
thah-pah-TEE-yahs

**translator (n)**
el traductor (m)
la traductora (f)
trah-dook-TOR/ah

**transport (n)**
el transporte
trahns-POR-teh

**tray (n)**
la bandeja
bahn-DEH-Hah

**tree (n)**
el árbol
AR-bol

**triangle (n)**
el triángulo
tree-AHN-goo-lo

**trip (day trip) (n)**
la excursión
eks-koor-see-ON

**trolley (n)**
el carrito
kar-RREE-to

**tropical (adj)**
tropical
tro-pee-KAHL

**trouble (n)**
el problema
pro-BLEH-mah

**trousers (n)**
los pantalones
pahn-tah-LO-ness

**trowel (n)**
la paleta
pah-LEH-tah

**truck (n)**
el camión
kah-mee-YON

**true (adj)**
verdadero (m)
bair-dah-DEH-ro

trunk
la trompa

turkey
el pavo

**trunk (animal) (n)**
la **trompa**
*TROM-pah*

**trunk (tree) (n)**
el **tronco**
*TRON-ko*

**trunks (n)**
el **bañador**
*bah-n'yah-DOR*

**T-shirt (n)**
la **camiseta**
*kah-mee-SEH-tah*

**tube (n)**
el **tubo**
*TOO-bo*

**tunnel (n)**
el **túnel**
*TOO-nel*

**turkey (n)**
el **pavo**
*PAH-bo*

**turtle (n)**
la **tortuga (marina)**
*tor-TOO-gah*
*(mah-REE-nah)*

**turn (n)**
el **turno**
*TOOR-no*

**twice (adv)**
**dos veces**
*doss BEH-thehs*

**twin (n)**
el **gemelo**
*Heh-MEH-lo*

**tyre (n)**
el **neumático**
*neh'oo-MAH-tee-ko*

# U

**ugly (adj)**
**feo (m)**
*FEH-o*

**umbrella (n)**
el **paraguas**
*pah-RAH-goo'ahs*

**uncle (n)**
el **tío**
*TEE-o*

**under (prep)**
**debajo de**
*deh-BAH-Ho deh*

**underground (adj)**
**subterráneo (m)**
*soob-ter-RRAH-nee-o*

**underground railway (n)**
el **metro**
*MEH-tro*

**underwear (n)**
la **ropa interior**
*RRO-pah in-teh-ree-OR*

**unfair (adj)**
**injusto (m)**
*in-HOOS-to*

**uniform (n)**
el **uniforme**
*oo-nee-FOR-meh*

umbrella
el paraguas

uniform
el uniforme

**universe (n)**
el **universo**
*oo-nee-BAIR-so*

**until (prep)**
**hasta**
*AHS-tah*

**unusual (adj)**
**poco común**
*PO-ko ko-MOON*

**upside down (adv)**
**al revés**
*ahl rreh-BESS*

**upstairs (adv)**
**arriba**
*ah-RREE-bah*

**useful (adj)**
**útil**
*OO-til*

**usually (adv)**
**generalmente**
*Hen-eh-rahl-MEN-teh*

# V

**van (n)**
la **camioneta**
*kah-mee-o-NEH-tah*

**vegetable (n)**
la **verdura**
*bair-DOO-rah*

**verb (n)**
el **verbo**
*BAIR-bo*

**very (adv)**
**muy**
*moo'e*

**vest (n)**
la **camiseta de tirantes**
*kah-mee-SEH-tah deh tee-RAHN-tess*

**vet (n)**
la **veterinaria (f)**
el **veterinario (m)**
*beh-teh-ree-NAH-ree-ah/o*

**video game (n)**
el **videojuego**
*be-deh-o-Hoo'EH-go*

**video player (n)**
el **reproductor de vídeo**
*reh-pro-dook-TOR deh BE-dee-o*

**village (n)**
la **aldea**
*AHL-deh-ah*

**violin (n)**
el **violín**
*be-o-LIN*

violin
el violín

A B C D E F G H I J K L M N O P Q R S **T U V** W X Y Z

91

**waist (n)**
la cintura
*thin-TOO-rah*

**waiter (n)**
el camarero
*kah-mah-REH-ro*

**waitress (n)**
la camarera
*kah-mah-REH-rah*

**walk (n)**
el camino
*kah-MEE-no*

**wall (n)**
el muro
*MOO-ro*

**war (n)**
la guerra
*GAIR-rrah*

**wardrobe (n)**
el armario
*ar-MAH-ree-o*

**warm (drink) (adj)**
templado (m)
*tem-PLAH-do*

**warm (weather) (adj)**
cálido (m)
*KAH-lee-do*

**warning (n)**
la advertencia
*ad-bair-TEN-thi-ah*

**washbasin (n)**
el lavabo
*lah-BAH-bo*

**washing (n)**
la colada
*ko-LAH-dah*

watering can
la regadera

**washing machine (n)**
la lavadora
*lah-bah-DOR-ah*

**wasp (n)**
la avispa
*ah-BISS-pah*

**watch (n)**
el reloj
*rreh-LOH*

**water (n)**
el agua
*AH-goo-ah*

**water lily (n)**
el nenúfar
*neh-NOO-far*

**watering can (n)**
la regadera
*reh-gah-DEH-rah*

**watermelon (n)**
la sandía
*sahn-DEE-ah*

**wave (n)**
la ola
*O-lah*

**wax (n)**
la cera
*THEH-rah*

**way in (n)**
la entrada
*en-TRAH-dah*

**way out (n)**
la salida
*sah-LEE-dah*

**we (pron)**
nosotras (f)
nosotros (m)
*nos-O-trahs/tros*

**weather (n)**
el tiempo
*tee-EM-po*

**website (n)**
el sitio web
*SEE-tee-o*

**weed (n)**
la mala hierba
*MAH-lah ee-AIR-bah*

**week (n)**
la semana
*seh-MAH-nah*

**weekend (n)**
el fin de semana
*fin deh seh-MAH-nah*

**welcome (adj)**
bienvenido (m)
*be-en-beh-NEE-do*

**wellington boots (n)**
las catiuscas
*kah-tee-OOS-kahs*

**west (n)**
el oeste
*o-ESS-teh*

**wet (adj)**
mojado (m)
*mo-HAH-do*

**whale (n)**
la ballena
*bah-YEH-nah*

**what (pron)**
qué
*keh*

**wheat (n)**
el trigo
*TREE-go*

**wheel (n)**
la rueda
*roo-EH-dah*

**wheelbarrow (n)**
la carretilla
*kar-rreh-TEE-yah*

**wheelchair (n)**
la silla de ruedas
*SEE-yah deh roo-EH-dahs*

**when (adv)**
cuándo
*koo'AHN-do*

**where (adv)**
dónde
*DON-deh*

**which (pron)**
cuál
*koo'ahl*

**while (conj)**
mientras
*mee-EN-trahs*

**whisker (n)**
el bigote
*be-GO-teh*

wave
la ola

A B C D E F G H I J K L M N O P Q R S T U V V W X Y Z

wing
el ala

**white (adj)**
blanco
*BLAHN-ko*

**who (pron)**
quién
*kee-EN*

**why (adv)**
por qué
*por KEH*

**wide (adj)**
ancho
*AHN-cho*

**wife (n)**
la mujer
*moo-HAIR*

**wild (adj)**
salvaje
*sahl-BAH-Heh*

**wind (n)**
el viento
*be-EN-to*

**windmill (n)**
el molino de viento
*mo-LEE-no deh be-EN-to*

**window (n)**
la ventana
*ben-TAH-nah*

**windy (adj)**
ventoso
*ben-TO-so*

**wing (n)**
el ala
*AH-lah*

**winner (n)**
el ganador (m)
la ganadora (f)
*gah-nah-DOR/ah*

**winter (n)**
el invierno
*in-be-AIR-no*

**with (prep)**
con
*kon*

**without (prep)**
sin
*sin*

**wolf (n)**
el lobo
*LO-bo*

**woman (n)**
la mujer
*moo-HAIR*

**wood (n)**
la madera
*mah-DEH-rah*

**wooden (adj)**
de madera
*deh mah-DEH-rah*

**wool (n)**
la lana
*LAH-nah*

**woolly hat (n)**
el gorro de lana
*GOR-rro deh LAH-nah*

**word (n)**
la palabra
*pah-LAH-brah*

**world (n)**
el mundo
*MOON-do*

**worm (n)**
la lombriz
*lom-BREETH*

**worse (adj)**
peor (sing)
peores (plu)
*PEH-or/peh-O-res*

**writing (n)**
la escritura
*ess-kree-TOO-rah*

# Y

yacht
el yate

**yacht (n)**
el yate
*YAH-teh*

**year (n)**
el año
*AH-n'yo*

**yellow (adj)**
amarillo (m)
*ah-mah-REE-yo*

**yesterday (adv)**
ayer
*ah-YAIR*

**yoghurt (n)**
el yogur
*yo-GOOR*

**you (pron)**
tú, usted, ustedes,
vosotros
*too/oo-STED/
oo-STEH-des/
boss-O-tross*

**young (adj)**
joven
*HO-ben*

**your (adj)**
tu, tus
*too/toos*

# Z

zebra
la cebra

**zebra (n)**
la cebra
*THEH-brah*

**zebra crossing (n)**
el paso de cebra
*PAH-so deh THEH-brah*

**zip (n)**
la cremallera
*kreh-mah-YEH-rah*

**zone (n)**
la zona
*THO-nah*

**zoo (n)**
el zoo
*THO-o*

zip
la cremallera

A
B
C
D
E
F
G
H
I
J
K
L
M
N
O
P
Q
R
S
T
U
V
**W**
X
**Y**
**Z**

# Spanish A–Z

In this section, Spanish words are in alphabetical order. They are followed by the English translation and a few letters to indicate what type of word it is – a noun (n) or adjective (adj), for example. Look at p56 to see a list of the different types of words.

Nouns in Spanish are either masculine or feminine. We have used (m) and (f) to tell you which they are. Sometimes a word in Spanish might mean more than one thing in English, so there might be two translations underneath.

Most of the nouns (naming words) here describe just one thing so they are singular. To make a noun plural (for more than one thing) you usually just add an "s" – the same as in English. In Spanish though, the other words in the sentence change too – *el* becomes *los* and *la* becomes *las*. The adjectives also change, usually getting an extra "s" at the end. In Spanish, an adjective usually comes after the noun.

**a, al (a + el) (prep)**
to

**a lo mejor (adv)**
maybe

**a menudo (adv)**
often

**a través de (prep)**
across

**abajo (adv)**
downstairs

**abajo (prep)**
under

**abarrotado (adj)**
crowded

**abeja (n) (f)**
bee

**abierto (adj)**
open

**abrigo (n) (m)**
coat

**abuelo/a (n) (m/f)**
grandfather/
grandmother

**abuelos (n) (m)**
grandparents

**aburrido (adj)**
boring

**acantilado (n) (m)**
cliff

**accidente (n) (m)**
accident

**aceite (n) (m)**
oil

**acera (n) (f)**
pavement

**actividad (n) (f)**
activity

**adelante (adv)**
forward

**adornos (n) (m)**
decorations

**adulto/a (n) (m/f)**
adult

**advertencia (n) (f)**
warning

**aeropuerto (n) (m)**
airport

**afilado (adj)**
sharp

**afortunado (adj)**
lucky

**afuera (adv)**
outside

**agenda (n) (f)**
diary

**agricultor/a (n) (m/f)**
farmer

**agua (n) (m)**
water

**aguacate (n) (m)**
avocado

**águila (n) (m)**
eagle

**aguja (n) (f)**
needle

**agujero (n) (m)**
hole

**ahí (adv)**
over there

**ahora (adv)**
now

**aire (n) (m)**
air

**ajedrez (n) (m)**
chess

**ajustado (adj)**
tight

**al revés (adv)**
upside down

**ala (n) (m)**
wing

**ala delta (n) (m)**
hang-glider

**aldea (n) (f)**
village

**alemán (n) (m)**
German

**aleta (n) (f)**
fin, flipper

**alfabeto (n) (m)**
alphabet

**alfombra (n) (f)**
rug

**alfombrilla (n) (f)**
mouse mat

**alga (n) (m)**
seaweed

**algo (pron)**
anything, something

**algodón (n) (m)**
cotton

**alguien (pron)**
anybody, someone

**algunas veces (adv)**
sometimes

**alguna, alguno, algunas, algunos (adj)**
some

**allá, allí (adv)**
there

**almohada (n) (f)**
pillow

**alrededor (prep)**
around

**alto (adj)**
high, loud, tall

**alubias (n) (f)**
beans

**alumno/a (n) (m/f)**
pupil

**amable (adj)**
kind (gentle)

**amarillo (adj)**
yellow

**ambulancia (n) (f)**
ambulance

**amigo/a (n) (m/f)**
friend

**ancho (adj)**
wide

**ancla (n) (m)**
anchor

**andén (n) (m)**
platform

**anillo (n) (m)**
ring

**animal (n) (m)**
animal

**animal de compañía (n) (m)**
pet

**año (n) (m)**
year

**antena (n) (f)**
antenna

**antes (prep)**
before

**apariencia (n) (f)**
appearance

**apartamento (n) (m)**
apartment

**aproximadamente (adv)**
about

**aquél, aquélla (pron)**
that one

**araña (n) (f)**
spider

**árbol (n) (m)**
tree

**arbusto (n) (m)**
bush

**arco (n) (m)**
arch

**arco iris (n) (m)**
rainbow

**ardilla (n) (f)**
squirrel

**área (n) (m)**
area

**arena (n) (f)**
sand

**armario (n) (m)**
cupboard, wardrobe

**arrecife (n) (m)**
reef

**arrecife de coral (n) (m)**
coral reef

**arriba (adv)**
upstairs

**arroz (n) (m)**
rice

**arte (n) (m)**
art

**artista (n) (m/f)**
artist

**ascensor (n) (m)**
lift

**asistente (n) (m/f)**
assistant

**áspero (adj)**
rough

**astronauta (n) (m/f)**
astronaut

**astrónomo/a (n) (m/f)**
astronomer

**asustado (adj)**
frightened

**ático (n) (m)**
attic

**atlas (n) (m)**
atlas

**atletismo (n) (m)**
athletics

**aula (n) (m)**
classroom

**autobús (n) (m)**
bus, coach

**autopista (n) (f)**
motorway

**aventura (n) (f)**
adventure

**avión (n) (m)**
aeroplane, plane

**avispa (n) (f)**
wasp

**¡ay!**
ouch!

**ayer (adv)**
yesterday

**ayuda (n) (f)**
help

**azúcar (n) (m)**
sugar

**azul (adj)**
blue

# B

**babuino (n) (m)**
baboon

**bádminton (n) (m)**
badminton

**bailarín/a (n) (m/f)**
ballet dancer, dancer

**baile (n) (m)**
dancing

**bajo (adj)**
low, short

**balcón (n) (m)**
balcony

**ballena (n) (f)**
whale

**balón (n) (m)**
ball

**balón de fútbol (n) (m)**
football (ball)

**baloncesto (n) (m)**
basketball

**bañador (n) (m)**
swimsuit, trunks

**banco (n) (m)**
bank (money), bench

**banda (n) (f)**
band

**bandeja (n) (f)**
tray

**bandera (n) (f)**
flag

**baño (n) (m)**
bath, toilet (room)

**barato (adj)**
cheap

**barba (n) (f)**
beard

**barbacoa (n) (f)**
barbecue

**barbilla (n) (f)**
chin

**barco (n) (m)**
ship

**barco de pesca (n) (m)**
fishing boat

**barco de vela (n) (m)**
sailing boat

**barra de labios (n) (f)**
lipstick

**barro (n) (m)**
mud

**basura (n) (f)**
rubbish

**batalla (n) (f)**
battle

**bate (n) (m)**
bat (sport)

**bateria (n) (f)**
drum kit

**batido (n) (m)**
milk shake

**bebé (n) (m)**
baby

**bebida (n) (f)**
drink

**béisbol (n) (m)**
baseball

**belleza (n) (f)**
beauty

**bello (adj)**
beautiful

**beso (n) (m)**
kiss

**biblioteca (n) (f)**
library

**bici (n) (f)**
bike

**bicicleta de montaña (n) (f)**
mountain bike

**bicicleta estática (n) (f)**
exercise bike

**bien (adv)**
fine

**bienvenido (adj)**
welcome

**bigote (n) (m)**
moustache, whisker

**billete (n) (m)**
ticket

**billón**
billion

**blanco (adj)**
white

**blando (adj)**
soft (not hard)

**bloque de pisos (n) (m)**
flats (building)

**blusa (n) (f)**
blouse

**boca (n) (f)**
mouth

**bola de nieve (n) (f)**
snowball

**bolígrafo (n) (m)**
pen

**bolsa (n) (f)**
bag, pouch (animal)

**bolsa de la compra (n) (f)**
shopping bag

**bolsillo (n) (m)**
pocket

**bolso (n) (m)**
handbag

**bombero/a (n) (m/f)**
firefighter

**bonito (adj)**
pretty

**borde (n) (m)**
edge

**borroso (adj)**
faint (pale)

**bosque (n) (m)**
forest

**bota (n) (f)**
boot

**bote (n) (m)**
can, boat

**bote de pintura (n) (m)**
paint tin

**bote de remos (n) (m)**
rowing boat

**bote salvavidas (n) (m)**
lifeboat

**botella (n) (f)**
bottle

**botón (n) (m)**
button

**boya (n) (f)**
buoy

**brazalete (n) (m)**
bracelet

**brazo (n) (m)**
arm

**brécol (n) (m)**
broccoli

**brillante (adj)**
bright, shiny

**brisa (n) (f)**
breeze

**broma (n) (f)**
joke

**brújula (n) (f)**
compass

**buceo con tubo (n) (m)**
snorkelling

**bueno (adj)**
good, nice

**bufanda (n) (f)**
scarf

**búho (n) (m)**
owl

**bulbo (n) (m)**
bulb (plant)

**burbuja (n) (f)**
bubble

**buzón (n) (m)**
letter box, postbox

# C

**caballero (n) (m)**
gentleman, knight

**caballo (n) (m)**
horse

**cabeza (n) (f)**
head

**cabra (n) (f)**
goat

**cacahuete (n) (m)**
peanut

**cachorro (n) (m)**
puppy

**cáctus (n) (m)**
cactus

**cada (adj)**
each, every

**cadena (n) (f)**
chain

**cadera (n) (f)**
hip

**café (n) (m)**
coffee

**cafetería (n) (f)**
café

**caimán (n) (m)**
alligator

**caja (n) (f)**
box, checkout, till (cash register)

**caja de cerillas (n) (f)**
matchbox

**cajón (n) (m)**
drawer

**calabaza (n) (f)**
pumpkin

**calcetín (n) (m)**
sock

**calculadora (n) (f)**
calculator

**calendario (n) (m)**
calendar

**cálido (adj)**
warm (weather)

**caliente (adj)**
hot

**calle (n) (f)**
road, street

**calor (n) (m)**
heat

**cama (n) (f)**
bed

**cámara (n) (f)**
camera

**camarero/a (n) (m/f)**
waiter/waitress

**cambio (n) (m)**
change, exchange

**camello (n) (m)**
camel

**camino (n) (m)**
path, walk

**camión (n) (m)**
lorry, truck

**camioneta (n) (f)**
van

**camisa (n) (f)**
shirt

**camiseta (n) (f)**
T-shirt

**camiseta de tirantes (n) (f)**
vest

**campana (n) (f)**
bell (metal)

**campo (n) (m)**
countryside

**cangrejo (n) (m)**
crab

**canguro (n) (m)**
kangaroo

**canicas (n) (f)**
marbles (toy)

**canoa (n) (f)**
canoe

**cansado (adj)**
tired

**capa (n) (f)**
cloak, layer

**capital (n) (f)**
capital

**capucha (n) (f)**
hood

**cara (n) (f)**
face

**caracol (n) (m)**
snail

**carne (n) (f)**
flesh, meat

**caro (adj)**
expensive

**carrera (n) (f)**
race

**carretilla (n) (f)**
wheelbarrow

**carrito (n) (m)**
trolley

**carro (n) (m)**
cart

**carrusel (n) (m)**
roundabout

**carta (n) (f)**
letter (postal)

**cartas (n) (f)**
cards

**cartera del colegio (n) (f)**
school bag

**cartero (n) (m)**
postman

**cartón (n) (m)**
cardboard

**casa (n) (f)**
home, house

**casado (adj)**
married

**casco (n) (m)**
helmet

**casi (adv)**
almost, nearly

**castillo de arena (n) (m)**
sandcastle

**catiuscas (n) (f)**
wellington boots

**CD (n) (m)**
CD

**cebolla (n) (f)**
onion

**cebra (n) (f)**
zebra

**ceja (n) (f)**
eyebrow

**cena (n) (f)**
dinner

**centro (n) (m)**
centre, middle

**cepillo de dientes (n) (m)**
toothbrush

**cepillo del pelo (n) (m)**
hairbrush

**cera (n) (f)**
crayon, wax

**cerca (adv)**
close, near

**cerdo (n) (m)**
pig

**cereales (n) (m)**
cereal

**cerebro (n) (m)**
brain

**cerrado (adj)**
closed

**césped (n) (m)**
grass, lawn

**cesta (n) (f)**
basket

**champiñón (n) (m)**
mushroom

**champú (n) (m)**
shampoo

**chapa (n) (f)**
badge

**chaqueta (n) (f)**
jacket

**chef (n) (m/f)**
chef

**chicle (n) (m)**
chewing gum

**chimenea (n) (f)**
chimney

**chimpancé (n) (m)**
chimpanzee

**chincheta (n) (f)**
drawing pin

**chocolate (n) (m)**
chocolate

**chocolate caliente (n) (m)**
hot chocolate

**ciclismo (n) (m)**
cycling

**ciego (adj)**
blind

**cielo (n) (m)**
sky

**ciencia (n) (f)**
science

**científico/a (n) (m/f)**
scientist

**ciervo (n) (m)**
deer

**cine (n) (m)**
cinema

**cinta (n) (f)**
cassette

**cinta métrica (n) (f)**
tape measure

**cintura (n) (f)**
waist

**cinturón (n) (m)**
belt

**circo (n) (m)**
circus

**círculo (n) (m)**
circle

**cisne (n) (m)**
swan

**ciudad (n) (f)**
city

**claro (adj)**
clear

**cliente (n) (m/f)**
customer

**clip (n) (m)**
paper clip

**coche (n) (m)**
car

**coche de bomberos (n) (m)**
fire engine

**coche de carreras (n) (m)**
racing car

**coche de juguete (n) (m)**
toy car

**coche de la policía (n) (m)**
police car

**cochecito (n) (m)**
buggy

**cocina (n) (f)**
cooker, cooking, kitchen

**coco (n) (m)**
coconut

**cocodrilo (n) (m)**
crocodile

**código postal (n) (m)**
postcode

**codo (n) (m)**
elbow

**cohete (n) (m)**
rocket

**cohete espacial (n) (m)**
space rocket

**cojín (n) (m)**
cushion

**cola (n) (f)**
queue, tail

**colada (n) (f)**
washing

**coleccionismo (n) (m)**
collecting

**colegio (n) (m)**
college

**colibrí (n) (m)**
hummingbird

**colina (n) (f)**
hill

**collar (n) (m)**
collar, necklace

**colmena (n) (f)**
hive

**color (n) (m)**
colour

**colorido (adj)**
colourful

**columpio (n) (m)**
swing

**combustible (n) (m)**
fuel

**comedor (n) (m)**
dining room

**cometa (n) (f)**
kite

**comida (n) (f)**
food, lunch, meal

**cómo (adv)**
how

**como (prep)**
like

**cómoda (n) (f)**
chest of drawers

**cómodo (adj)**
comfortable

**compañero/a (n) (m/f)**
partner

**comprador/a (n) (m/f)**
shopper

**con (prep)**
with

**concha (n) (f)**
shell

**concierto (n) (m)**
concert

**conejillo de indias (n) (m)**
guinea pig

**conejo (n) (m)**
rabbit

**congelador (n)**
freezer

**consulta (n) (f)**
surgery (doctor's)

**continente (n)**
continent

**contrarios (adj)**
opposites

**control remoto (n) (m)**
remote control

**copo de nieve (n) (m)**
snowflake

**corazón (n) (m)**
heart

**corbata (n) (f)**
tie

**corcho (n) (m)**
cork

**cordero (n) (m)**
lamb

**corona (n) (f)**
crown

**correcto (adj)**
correct, right

**correo (n) (m)**
mail

**correo electrónico (n) (m)**
email

**cortacésped (n) (m)**
lawn mower

**cortina (n) (f)**
curtain

**cosa (n) (f)**
thing

**cosecha (n) (f)**
crop, harvest

**cosechadora (n) (f)**
combine harvester

**costa (n) (f)**
coast, seaside

**crema solar (n) (f)**
suncream

**cremallera (n) (f)**
zip

**crepe (n) (m)**
pancake

**criatura (n) (f)**
creature

**cruce (n) (m)**
crossing

**cruz (n) (f)**
tick

**cuaderno de ejercicios (n) (m)**
exercise book

**cuadrado (n) (m)**
square

**cuadro (n) (m)**
painting, picture

**cuál (pron)**
which

**cuándo (adv)**
when

**cuarto (n) (m)**
quarter

**cuarto de baño (n) (m)**
bathroom

**cubito de hielo (n) (m)**
ice cube

**cubo (n) (m)**
bucket, cube

**cubo de la basura (n) (m)**
bin (rubbish)

**cuchara (n) (f)**
spoon

**cuchillo (n) (m)**
knife

**cuello (n) (m)**
neck

**cuenco (n) (m)**
bowl

**cuenta (n) (f)**
bead, bill

**cuerda (n) (f)**
rope, skipping rope, string

**cuerno (n) (m)**
horn

**cuero (n) (m)**
leather

**cuerpo (n) (m)**
body

**cueva (n) (f)**
cave

**cuidadoso (adj)**
careful

**cumbre (n) (f)**
top (not bottom)

**cumpleaños (n) (m)**
birthday

**cúpula (n) (f)**
dome

**curioso (adj)**
curious

**curvo (adj)**
curved

# D

**dado (n) (m)**
dice

**de (prep)**
about, from

**de, del (de + el) (prep)**
of

**de fuera (adj)**
away

**de madera (adj)**
wooden

**de más (adj)**
extra

**de moda (adj)**
fashionable

**de repente (adv)**
suddenly

**de verdad (adv)**
really

**debajo de (prep)**
below, under

**deberes (n) (m)**
homework

**dedo (n) (m)**
finger

**dedo del pie (n) (m)**
toe

**delfín (n) (m)**
dolphin

**delgado (adj)**
thin

**delicioso (adj)**
delicious

**demasiado (adv)**
too

**dentista (n) (m/f)**
dentist

**dentro, dentro de (prep)**
inside

**dependiente/a (n) (m/f)**
shop assistant

**deporte (n) (m)**
sport

**derecha (adj)**
right (not left)

**desafío (n) (m)**
challenge

**desayuno (n) (m)**
breakfast

**descanso (n) (m)**
break

**descubrimiento (n) (m)**
discovery

**desfile (n) (m)**
parade

**desierto (n) (m)**
desert

**desorden (n) (m)**
mess

**despacio (adv)**
slowly

**despertador (n) (m)**
alarm clock

**después de (prep)**
after

**detrás de (prep)**
behind

**día (n) (m)**
day

**diagrama (n) (m)**
diagram

**dibujo (n) (m)**
drawing

**diccionario (n)**
dictionary

**diente (n) (m)**
tooth

**diente de león (n) (m)**
dandelion

**diferente (adj)**
different

**difícil (adj)**
difficult

**digital (adj)**
digital

**diminuto (adj)**
tiny

**dinero (n) (m)**
money

**dinero de bolsillo (n) (m)**
pocket money

**dinero (en efectivo) (n) (m)**
cash

**dinosaurio (n) (m)**
dinosaur

**Dios (n) (m)**
God

**dirección (n) (f)**
address, direction

**dirección electrónica (n) (f)**
email address

**directamente (adv)**
directly

**discapacitado (adj)**
disabled

**disco duro (n) (m)**
hard drive

**discoteca (n) (f)**
disco

**discurso (n) (m)**
speech

**diseño (n) (m)**
pattern

**disfraz (n) (m)**
fancy dress

**distancia (n) (f)**
distance

**diversión (n) (f)**
fun

**divorciado (adj)**
divorced

**dolor de cabeza (n) (m)**
headache

**dolor de oídos (n) (m)**
earache

**dónde (adv)**
where

**dos veces (adv)**
twice

**dragón (n) (m)**
dragon

**ducha (n) (f)**
shower

**dulce (n) (m)**
sweet

**dulce (adj)**
gentle

**durante (prep)**
during

**duro (adj)**
hard

**DVD (n) (m)**
DVD

# E

**e (before "i" or "hi")(conj)**
and

**eco (n) (m)**
echo

**ecuador (n) (m)**
equator

**edad (n) (f)**
age

**edificio (n) (m)**
building

**edredón (n) (m)**
duvet

**efecto (n) (m)**
effect

**ejercicio (n) (m)**
exercise

**ejército (n) (m)**
army

**el (article) (m)**
the

**él (pron)**
he

**eléctrica (adj)**
electrical

**elefante (n) (m)**
elephant

**ella (pron)**
she

**ellas (pron) (f),
ellos (pron) (m/f)**
they

**embarrado (adj)**
muddy

**emergencia (n) (f)**
emergency

**emocionado (adj)**
excited

**en (prep)**
in, into, on

**en forma (adj)**
fit

**en todas partes (adv)**
everywhere

**enciclopedia (n) (f)**
encyclopedia

**encima de (prep)**
above, on top of

**enfadado (adj)**
angry

**enfermedad (n) (f)**
illness

**enfermero/a (n) (m/f)**
nurse

**enfermo (adj)**
ill, sick

**enfrente de (prep)**
opposite

**enorme (adj)**
huge

**ensalada (n) (f)**
salad

**entonces (conj)**
then

**entrada (n) (f)**
entrance, way in

**entre (prep)**
between

**entusiasta (adj)**
enthusiastic

**equipaje (n) (m)**
luggage

**equipo (n) (m)**
equipment, team

**equitación (n) (f)**
horse riding, riding

**error (n) (m)**
mistake

**escalera (n) (f)**
ladder, stairs

**escurabajo (n) (m)**
beetle

**escoba (n) (f)**
broom

**escondite (n) (m)**
hide-and-seek

**escritorio (n) (m)**
desk

**escritura (n) (f)**
writing

**escuela (n) (f)**
school

**espacio (n) (m)**
space

**espalda (n) (f)**
back (body)

**español (n) (m)**
Spanish

**espantoso (adj)**
frightening

**especial (adj)**
special

**espectáculo (n) (m)**
show

**espejo (n) (m)**
mirror

**esponja (n) (f)**
sponge

**esqueleto (n) (m)**
skeleton

**esquí (n) (m)**
ski, skiing

**esquina (n) (f)**
corner

**esta, este (adj) (f/m)**
this

**esta noche (adv)**
tonight

**estación (n) (f)**
season, station

**estación de tren (n) (f)**
railway station

**estanque (n) (m)**
pond

**estante (n) (m)**
shelf

**este (n) (m)**
east

**esterilla (n) (f)**
mat

**estómago (n) (m)**
stomach

**estonces (conj)**
then

**estrecho (adj)**
narrow

**estrella (n) (f)**
star

**estrella de cine (n) (f)**
film star

**estrella de mar (n) (f)**
starfish

**estricto (adj)**
strict

**estuche (n) (m)**
pencil case

**estudiante (n) (m/f)**
student

**estupendo (adj)**
great (good)

**estúpido (adj)**
stupid

**evento (n) (m)**
event

**exámen (n) (m)**
exam

**excelente (adj)**
excellent

**excursión (n) (f)**
trip (day trip)

**expedición (n) (f)**
expedition

**experimento (n) (m)**
experiment

**experto/a (n) (m/f)**
expert

**explorador/a (n) (m/f)**
explorer

**explosión (n) (f)**
explosion

**extinto (adj)**
extinct

**extranjero (adj)**
foreign

**extremadamente (adv)**
extremely

# F

**fábrica (n) (f)**
factory

**fabuloso (adj)**
fabulous

**fácil (adj)**
easy

**falda (n) (f)**
skirt

**falso (adj)**
false

**familia (n) (f)**
family

**famoso (adj)**
famous

**fantástico (adj)**
fantastic

**farmacia (n) (f)**
chemist (shop)

**faro (n) (m)**
lighthouse

**farola (n) (f)**
street light

**favorito (adj)**
favourite

**fecha (n) (f)**
date

**feliz (adj)**
happy

**feo (adj)**
ugly

**feria (n) (f)**
fair

**ferry (n) (m)**
ferry

**festival (n) (m)**
festival

**fideo (n) (m)**
noodle

**fieltro (n) (m)**
felt

**fiesta (n) (f)**
party

**fin (n) (m)**
end

**fin de semana (n) (m)**
weekend

**flauta (n) (f)**
flute

**flecha (n) (f)**
arrow

**flojo (adj)**
loose

**flor (n) (f)**
flower

**foca (n) (f)**
seal

**fondo (n) (m)**
bottom

**forma (n) (f)**
shape

**forro polar (n) (m)**
fleece (jacket)

**fósil (n) (m)**
fossil

**foto (n) (f)**
photo

**frambuesa (n) (f)**
raspberry

**francés (n) (m)**
French

**frase (n) (f)**
phrase

**fregadero (n) (m)**
sink (kitchen)

**fresa (n) (f)**
strawberry

**fresco (adj)**
cool, fresh

**frigorífico (n) (m)**
fridge

**frío (adj)**
cold

**fruta (n) (f)**
fruit

**fuego (n) (m)**
fire

**fuera de (prep)**
out of

**fuerte (adj)**
strong

**fútbol (n) (m)**
football (game)

**futuro (n) (m)**
future

# G

**gafas (n) (f)**
glasses

**gafas de nadar (n) (f)**
goggles

**gafas de sol (n) (f)**
sunglasses

**galleta (n) (f)**
biscuit

**ganador/a (n) (m/f)**
winner

**garaje (n) (m)**
garage

**garra (n) (f)**
claw

**garza real (n) (f)**
heron

**gas (n) (m)**
gas

# gasolina • petrol

**gasolina (n) (f)**
petrol

**gatito (n) (m)**
kitten

**gato (n) (m)**
cat

**gaviota (n) (f)**
seagull

**gemelo (n) (m)**
twin

**generalmente (adv)**
usually

**gente (n) (f)**
people

**gigante (n) (m)**
giant

**gimnasia (n) (f)**
gymnastics

**girasol (n) (m)**
sunflower

**globo (n) (m)**
balloon, globe

**globo aerostático (n) (m)**
hot-air balloon

**gobierno (n) (m)**
government

**gol (n) (m)**
goal

**golf (n) (m)**
golf

**goma (n) (f)**
rubber band

**goma de borrar (n) (f)**
rubber (eraser)

**gordo (adj)**
fat

**gorila (n) (m)**
gorilla

**gorra (n) (f)**
cap

**gorro de lana (n) (m)**
woolly hat

**gota (n) (f)**
drop

**grande (adj)**
big

**granero (n) (m)**
barn

**granja (n) (f)**
farm

**grifo (n) (m)**
tap

**grúa (n) (f)**
crane

**grueso (adj)**
thick

**grupo (n) (m)**
group

**guante (n) (m)**
glove

**guante del horno (n) (m)**
oven glove

**guardería (n) (f)**
nursery

**guepardo (n) (m)**
cheetah

**guerra (n) (f)**
war

**guía (n) (f)**
guide

**guisante (n) (m)**
pea

**guitarra (n) (f)**
guitar

# H

**habitación (n) (f)**
bedroom, room

**hábitat (n) (m)**
habitat

**hacia (prep)**
towards

**hacia atrás (adv)**
backwards

**halcón (n) (m)**
hawk

**hambriento (adj)**
hungry

**hámster (n) (m)**
hamster

**harina (n) (f)**
flour

**hasta (prep)**
until

**hecho (n) (m)**
fact

**helado (n) (m)**
ice cream

**helecho (n) (m)**
fern

**helicóptero (n) (m)**
helicopter

**helicóptero de la policía (n) (m)**
police helicopter

**herida (n) (f)**
injury

**hermano/a (n) (m/f)**
brother/sister

**héroe (n) (m)**
hero

**herramienta (n) (f)**
tool

**hervidor de agua (n) (m)**
kettle

**hielo (n) (m)**
ice

**hija (n) (f)**
daughter

**historia (n) (f)**
history, story

**histórico (adj)**
historical

**hobby (n) (m)**
hobby

**hockey (n) (m)**
hockey

**hockey sobre hielo (n) (m)**
ice hockey

**hoja (n) (m)**
leaf

**hola**
hello, hi

**hombre (n) (m)**
man

**hombro (n) (m)**
shoulder, shoulder bone

**hora (n) (f)**
hour, time (What time is it?)

**hora de la comida (n) (f)**
lunch break

**hora del recreo (n) (f)**
playtime

**horario (n) (m)**
timetable

**horas de apertura (n) (f)**
opening hours

**hormiga (n) (f)**
ant

**horno (n) (m)**
oven

**horrible (adj)**
horrible

**hospital (n) (m)**
hospital

**hotel (n) (m)**
hotel

**hoy (adv)**
today

**hueso (n) (m)**
bone

**huevo (n) (m)**
egg

**humano (n) (m)**
human

**humo (n) (m)**
smoke

**huracán (n) (m)**
hurricane

# I

**idea (n) (f)**
idea

**idioma (n) (m)**
language

**iglesia (n) (f)**
church

**igual (adj)**
equal

**imán (n) (m)**
magnet

**impermeable (n) (m)**
raincoat

**importante (adj)**
important

**imposible (adj)**
impossible

**incluso (adv)**
even

**increible (adj)**
amazing

**información (n) (f)**
information

**informe (n) (m)**
report

**inglés (n) (m)**
English

**ingrediente (n) (m)**
ingredient

**injusto (adj)**
unfair

**inmediatamente (adv)**
immediately

**inodoro (n) (m)**
toilet

**insecto (n) (m)**
insect

**instrucción (n) (f)**
instruction

**instrumento (n) (m)**
instrument

**interesante (adj)**
interesting

**internacional (adj)**
international

**Internet (n) (m)**
Internet

**inundación (n) (f)**
flood

**invernadero (n) (m)**
greenhouse

**invierno (n) (m)**
winter

**invitación (n) (f)**
invitation

**isla (n) (f)**
island

**izquierda (adj)**
left

# J

**jabón (n) (m)**
soap

**jardín (n) (m)**
garden

**jardinería (n) (f)**
gardening

**jardinero/a (n) (m/f)**
gardener

**jarra (n) (f)**
jug

**jaula (n) (f)**
cage

**jersey (n) (m)**
jumper, sweater

**jet (n) (m)**
jet

**jirafa (n) (f)**
giraffe

**joven (adj)**
young

**joya (n) (f)**
jewel

**joyas (n) (f)**
jewellery

**judo (n) (m)**
judo

**juego (n) (m)**
game

**juego de mesa (n) (m)**
board game

**Juegos Olímpicos (n) (m)**
Olympic Games

**jugador/a (n) (m/f)**
player

**juguete (n) (m)**
toy

**juntos (adv)**
together

**justo (adv)**
just

# K

**kárate (n) (m)**
karate

**koala (n) (m)**
koala

# L

**la (article) (f)**
the

**la (pron)**
her, it

**lagartija (n) (f)**
lizard

**lago (n) (m)**
lake

**lámpara (n) (f)**
lamp

**lana (n) (f)**
wool

**langosta (n) (f)**
lobster

**lápiz (n) (m)**
pencil

**lápiz de color (n) (m)**
coloured pencil

**largo (adj)**
long

**las (article) (f plu)**
the

**lavabo (n) (m)**
sink (bathroom), washbasin

**lavadora (n) (f)**
washing machine

**lazo (n) (m)**
ribbon

**le (pron)**
her, him

**lección (n) (f)**
lesson

**leche (n) (f)**
milk

**lechuga (n) (f)**
lettuce

**lectura (n) (f)**
reading

**lejos (adv)**
far

**lengua (n) (f)**
language, tongue

**lentamente (adv)**
slowly

**lento (adj)**
slow

**león (n) (m)**
lion

**león marino (n) (m)**
sea lion

**leopardo (n) (m)**
leopard

**letra (n) (f)**
letter (alphabet)

**libélula (n) (f)**
dragonfly

**librería (n) (f)**
bookshop

**libreta (n) (f)**
notebook

**libro (n) (m)**
book

**liebre (n) (f)**
hare

**ligero (adj)**
light (not heavy)

**limón (n) (m)**
lemon

**limonada (n) (f)**
lemonade

**limpio (adj)**
clean

**línea (n) (f)**
line

**linterna (n) (f)**
torch

**lirón (n) (m)**
dormouse

**lista (n) (f)**
list

**lista de la compra (n) (f)**
shopping list

**listo (adj)**
clever, ready

**llano (adj)**
flat

**llave (n) (f)**
key

**llegada (n) (f)**
arrival

**lleno (adj)**
full

**lluvia (n) (f)**
rain

**lo (pron)**
him, it

**lobo (n) (m)**
wolf

**lombriz (n) (f)**
earthworm, worm

**loro (n) (m)**
parrot

**los (article) (m plu)**
the

**luna (n) (f)**
moon

**lupa (n) (f)**
magnifying glass

**luz (n) (f)**
light

**luz solar (n) (f)**
sunlight

# M

**maceta (n)**
flowerpot

**madera (n) (f)**
wood

**madrastra (n) (f)**
stepmother

**madre (n) (f)**
mother

**maduro (adj)**
ripe

**magnético (adj)**
magnetic

**mago (n) (m)**
magician

**mala hierba (n) (f)**
weed

**maleta (n) (f)**
suitcase

**malo (adj)**
bad

**mamá (n) (f)**
mum

**mamífero (n) (m)**
mammal

**mañana (n) (f)**
morning

**mañana (adv)**
tomorrow

**mandil (n) (m)**
apron

**mandos (n) (m)**
controls

**manga (n) (f)**
sleeve

**mano (n) (f)**
hand

**manopla (n) (f)**
mitten

**manta (n) (f)**
blanket

**mantequilla (n) (f)**
butter

**manzana (n) (f)**
apple

**mapa (n) (m)**
map

**maquillaje (n) (m)**
make-up

**máquina (n) (f)**
machine

**mar (n) (m)**
sea

**marca (n) (f)**
mark

**marco (n) (m)**
frame

**marea (n) (f)**
tide

**margarita (n)**
daisy

**marido (n) (m)**
husband

**marinero (n) (m)**
sailor

**marioneta (n) (f)**
puppet

**mariposa (n) (f)**
butterfly

**mariquita (n) (f)**
ladybird

**marrón (adj)**
brown

**más de**
more than (numbers)

**más que**
more than

**máscara (n) (f)**
mask

**matemáticas (n) (f)**
maths

**mayoría (adj)**
most

**me (pron)**
me

**media (n) (f)**
stocking

**medianoche (n) (f)**
midnight

**medicina (n) (f)**
medicine

**médico/a (n) (m/f)**
doctor

**medida (n) (f)**
measurement

**medio ambiente (n) (m)**
environment

**medusa (n) (f)**
jellyfish

**mejor, mejores (adj) (sing/plu)**
better

**mejor (pron)**
best

**melón (n) (m)**
melon

**mensaje (n) (m)**
message

**mensaje de texto (n) (m)**
text message

**menú (n) (m)**
menu

**mercado (n) (m)**
market

**mermelada (n) (f)**
jam

**mes (n) (m)**
month

**mesa (n) (f)**
table

**metal (n) (m)**
metal

**metro (n) (m)**
underground railway

**mezcla (n) (f)**
mixture

**mezquita (n) (f)**
mosque

**mi (adj)**
my

**microondas (n) (m)**
microwave

**miel (n) (f)**
honey

**miembro (n) (m)**
member

**mientras (conj)**
while

**mil**
thousand

**millón**
million

**mineral (n) (m)**
mineral

**minuto (n) (m)**
minute

**mismo (adj)**
same

**mitad (n) (f)**
half

**mochila (n) (f)**
backpack, rucksack

**moda (n) (f)**
fashion

**mojado (adj)**
wet

**molino de viento (n) (m)**
windmill

**moneda (n) (f)**
coin

**monedero (n) (m)**
purse

**mono (n) (m)**
monkey

**monopatín (n) (m)**
skateboard

**monstruo (n) (m)**
monster

**montaña (n) (f)**
mountain

**moqueta (n) (f)**
carpet

**mosca (n) (f)**
fly

**motocicleta (n) (f)**
motorbike

**motonieve (n) (f)**
snowmobile

**motor (n) (m)**
motor

**mucho (adj)**
(a) lot

**muchos (adj)**
many

**muebles (n) (m)**
furniture

**muerto (adj)**
dead

**muesli (n) (m)**
muesli

**mujer (n) (f)**
female, wife, woman

**mundo (n) (m)**
world

**muñeca (n) (f)**
doll

**muñeco de nieve (n) (m)**
snowman

**murciélago (n) (m)**
bat (animal)

**muro (n) (m)**
wall

**museo (n) (m)**
museum

**música (n) (f)**
music

**músico (n) (m)**
musician

**muy (adv)**
very

# N

**nacional (adj)**
national

**nada (pron)**
nothing

**nadie (pron)**
nobody

**naranja (n) (f)**
orange (fruit)

**naranja (adj)**
orange (colour)

**nariz (n) (f)**
nose

**nata (n) (f)**
cream (food)

**natación (n) (f)**
swimming

**naturaleza (n) (f)**
nature

**navidades (n) (f)**
Christmas

**negocio (n) (m)**
business

**negro (adj)**
black

**nenúfar (n) (m)**
water lily

**neumático (n) (m)**
tyre

**nido (n) (m)**
nest

**niebla (n) (f)**
fog

**nieve (n) (f)**
snow

**ninguna parte (adv)**
nowhere

**niño/a (n) (m/f)**
boy/girl, child

**niños (n) (m)**
children

**nivelado (adj)**
level

**noche (n) (f)**
night

**nombre (n) (m)**
name

**norte (n) (m)**
north

**nosotras, nosotros (pron) (f/m)**
we

**nota (n) (f)**
note

**noticias (n) (f)**
news

**novio/a (n) (m/f)**
boyfriend/girlfriend

**nube (n) (f)**
cloud

**nublado (adj)**
cloudy

**nudo (n) (m)**
knot

**nuestro (adj)**
our

**nuevo (adj)**
new

**número (n) (m)**
number

**nunca (adv)**
never

# O

**o (conj)**
or

**objeto (n) (m)**
object

**obra (n) (f)**
play

**observación de aves (n) (f)**
bird-watching

**océano (n) (m)**
ocean

**ocupado (adj)**
busy

**oeste (n) (m)**
west

**oficina (n) (f)**
office

**oficina de correos (n) (f)**
post office

**ojo (n) (m)**
eye

**ola (n) (f)**
wave

**olla (n) (f)**
saucepan

**olor (n) (m)**
smell

**operación (n) (f)**
operation

**ordenador (n) (m)**
computer

**(ordenador) portátil (n) (m)**
laptop

**oreja (n) (f)**
ear

**orilla (n) (f)**
bank (river), shore

**oro (n) (m)**
gold

**orquesta (n) (f)**
orchestra

**oruga (n) (f)**
caterpillar

**oscuro (adj)**
dark

**osito de peluche (n) (m)**
teddy bear

**oso (n) (m)**
bear

**oso polar (n) (m)**
polar bear

**otoño (n) (m)**
autumn

**otra vez (adv)**
again

**otro (adj)**
other

**óvalo (n) (m)**
oval

**oveja (n) (f)**
sheep

# P

**paciente (n) (m/f)**
patient

**paciente (adj)**
patient

**padrastro (n) (m)**
stepfather

**padres (n) (m)**
parents

**página (n) (f)**
page

**país (n) (m)**
country

**paja (n) (f)**
hay

**pájaro (n) (m)**
bird

**pajita (n) (f)**
straw

**pala (n) (f)**
spade

**palabra (n) (f)**
word

**paleta (n) (f)**
trowel

**palmera (n) (f)**
palm tree

**palo (n) (m)**
stick

**pamela (n) (f)**
sunhat

**pan (n) (m)**
bread

**panadería (n) (f)**
bakery

**panda (n) (m)**
panda

**paño de cocina (n) (m)**
tea towel

**pantalla (n) (f)**
screen

**pantalones (n) (m)**
trousers

**pantalones cortos (n) (m)**
shorts

**pañuelo (n) (m)**
handkerchief

**pañuelos de papel (n) (m)**
tissues

**papá (n) (m)**
dad

**papel (n) (m)**
paper

**papel higiénico (n) (m)**
toilet paper

**par (n) (m)**
pair

**para (prep)**
for

**parada de autobús (n) (f)**
bus stop

**paraguas (n) (m)**
umbrella

**parque (n) (m)**
park

**parte (n) (f)**
part

**parte de atrás (adj)**
back (not front)

**partido (n) (m)**
match (sport)

**pasado (n) (m)**
past (history)

**pasajero/a (n) (m/f)**
passenger

**pasaporte (n) (m)**
passport

**paso (n) (m)**
step

**paso de cebra (n) (m)**
zebra crossing

**pasta (n) (f)**
pasta

**pasta de dientes (n) (f)**
toothpaste

**pastel (n) (m)**
cake

**pata (n) (f)**
paw

**patata (n) (f)**
potato

**patatas fritas (n) (f)**
chips

**patinaje (n) (m)**
skating

**patinaje en línea (n) (m)**
rollerblading

**patinaje sobre hielo (n) (m)**
ice skating

**patinaje sobre ruedas (n) (m)**
roller skating

**patio de recreo (n) (m)**
playground

**patito (n) (m)**
duckling

**pato (n) (m)**
duck

**pavo (n) (m)**
turkey

**payaso (n) (m)**
clown

**paz (n) (f)**
peace

**pecho (n) (m)**
chest

**pedal (n) (m)**
pedal

**pegajoso (adj)**
sticky

**pegamento (n) (m)**
glue

**pegatina (n) (f)**
sticker

**peine (n) (m)**
comb

**pelícano (n) (m)**
pelican

**película (n) (f)**
film

**peligro (n) (m)**
danger

**peligroso (adj)**
dangerous

**pelo (n) (m)**
fur, hair

**peludo (adj)**
hairy

**peluquería (n) (f)**
hairdresser's

**pendiente (n) (m)**
earring

**peor/peores (adj) (sing/plu)**
worse

**pequeño (adj)**
little, small

**pera (n) (f)**
pear

**percha (n) (f)**
coat hanger (clothes)

**perfecto (adj)**
perfect

**periódico (n) (m)**
newspaper

**pero (conj)**
but

**perrito caliente (n) (m)**
hot dog

**perro (n) (m)**
dog

**perro pastor (n) (m)**
sheepdog

**persona (n) (f)**
person

**persona mayor (n) (f)**
old person

**pesado (adj)**
heavy

**pesca (n) (f)**
fishing

**pestaña (n) (f)**
eyelash

**pez (n) (m)**
fish

**pez dorado (n) (m)**
goldfish

**piano (n) (m)**
piano

**picnic (n) (m)**
picnic

**pico (n) (m)**
beak

**pie (n) (m)**
foot

**piedra (n) (f)**
pebble, stone

**piel (n) (f)**
skin

**pierna (n) (f)**
leg

**pijama (n) (m)**
pyjamas

**pila (n) (f)**
battery

**piloto (n) (m/f)**
pilot

**pimienta (n) (f)**
pepper

**piña (n) (f)**
pineapple, pinecone

**pincel (n) (m)**
paintbrush

**pingüino (n) (m)**
penguin

**pino (n) (m)**
pine tree

**pintura (n) (f)**
paint, painting

**piscina (n) (f)**
swimming pool

**pizarra (n) (f)**
blackboard

**pizza (n) (f)**
pizza

**plancha (n) (f)**
iron (clothes)

**planeta (n) (m)**
planet

**planta (n) (f)**
plant

**plástico (adj)**
plastic

**plata (n) (f)**
silver

**plátano (n) (m)**
banana

**plato (n) (m)**
plate

**playa (n) (f)**
beach

**pluma (n) (f)**
feather

**pobre (adj)**
poor

**poco común (adj)**
unusual

**poco profundo (adj)**
shallow

**policía (n) (f)**
police

**polilla (n) (f)**
moth

**pollito (n) (m)**
chick

**pollo (n) (m)**
chicken

**polo (n) (m)**
ice lolly

**polvo (n) (m)**
dust, powder

**por (prep)**
through

**por delante de (prep)**
past

**por favor (adv)**
please

**por qué (adv)**
why

**porque (conj)**
because

**posible (adj)**
possible

**postal (n) (f)**
postcard

**póster (n) (m)**
poster

**postre (n) (m)**
dessert

**prado (n) (m)**
field

**precio (n) (m)**
price

**precioso (adj)**
lovely

**pregunta (n) (f)**
question

**premio (n) (m)**
prize

**presa (n) (f)**
dam

**presidente/a (n) (m/f)**
president

**primavera (n) (f)**
spring (season)

**primer ministro/a (n) (m/f)**
prime minister

**primero (adv)**
first

**primeros auxilios (n) (m)**
first aid

**primo/a (n) (m/f)**
cousin

**princesa (n) (f)**
princess

**principal (adj)**
main (adj)

**príncipe (n) (m)**
prince

**prismáticos (n) (m)**
binoculars

**probablemente (adv)**
probably

**problema (n) (m)**
problem, trouble

**productos lácteos (n) (m)**
dairy products

**profesor/a (n) (m/f)**
teacher

**profundo (adj)**
deep

**programa (n) (m)**
programme

**pronto (adv)**
soon

**propio (adj)**
own

**próximo (adj)**
next

**proyecto (n) (m)**
project

**pudín (n) (m)**
pudding

**pueblo (n) (m)**
town

**puente (n) (m)**
bridge

**puerta (n) (f)**
door

**puerta principal (n) (f)**
front door

**puerto (n) (m)**
harbour

**puesta de sol (n) (f)**
sunset

**pulgar (n) (m)**
thumb

**puño (n) (m)**
fist

**púrpura (adj)**
purple

# Q

**qué (pron)**
what

**querido (adj)**
dear (letter)

**queso (n) (m)**
cheese

**quién (pron)**
who

**quieto (adj)**
still

**quizás (adv)**
perhaps

# R

**radio (n) (f)**
radio

**raíz (n) (f)**
root

**rama (n) (f)**
branch

**rana (n) (f)**
frog

**rápidamente (adv)**
quickly

**rápido (adv)**
fast

**raqueta (n) (f)**
racket

**raro (adj)**
strange

**rascacielos (n) (m)**
skyscraper

**rastrillo (n) (m)**
rake

**rata (n) (f)**
rat

**ratón (n) (m)**
mouse (animal/computer)

**rayas (n) (f)**
stripes

**rebaño (n) (m)**
flock

**receta (n) (f)**
recipe

**recibidor (n) (m)**
hall

**recibo (n) (m)**
receipt

**rectángulo (n) (m)**
rectangle

**recto (adj)**
straight

**red (n) (f)**
net

**redondo (adj)**
round

**regadera (n) (f)**
watering can

**regalo (n) (m)**
present, souvenir

**regla (n) (f)**
ruler (measuring)

**reina (n) (f)**
queen

**relámpago (n) (m)**
lightning

**reloj (n) (m)**
clock, watch

**remo (n) (m)**
oar, rowing

**renacuajo (n) (m)**
tadpole

**reno (n) (m)**
reindeer

**repollo (n) (m)**
cabbage

**reproductor de CD (n) (m)**
CD player

**reproductor de DVD (n) (m)**
DVD player

**reproductor de vídeo (n) (m)**
video player

**rescate (n) (m)**
rescue

**respuesta (n) (f)**
answer

**restaurante (n) (m)**
restaurant

**resultado (n) (m)**
score

**revista (n) (f)**
magazine

**rey (n) (m)**
king

**rico (adj)**
rich

**rinoceronte (n) (m)**
rhinoceros

**río (n) (m)**
river

**rizado (adj)**
curly

**robot (n) (m)**
robot

**roca (n) (f)**
rock

**rodilla (n) (f)**
knee

**rojo (adj)**
red

**rombo (n) (m)**
diamond

**rompecabezas (n) (m)**
puzzle

**ropa (n) (f)**
clothes

**ropa interior (n) (f)**
underwear

**rosa (adj)**
pink

**rosa (n) (f)**
rose

**roto (adj)**
broken

**rotulador (n) (m)**
felt-tip pen

**rubio (adj)**
blonde

**rueda (n) (f)**
wheel

**rugby (n) (m)**
rugby

**ruidoso (adj)**
noisy

**ruta (n) (f)**
route

# S

**sábana (n) (f)**
sheet (bed)

**saco (n) (m)**
sack

**saco de dormir (n) (m)**
sleeping bag

**sal (n) (f)**
salt

**salida (n) (f)**
way out

**salón (n) (m)**
living room

**saltamontes (n) (m)**
grasshopper

**salvaje (adj)**
wild

**salvavidas (n) (m)**
life jacket

**sandalia (n) (f)**
sandal

**sandía (n) (f)**
watermelon

**sándwich (n) (m)**
sandwich

**sangre (n) (f)**
blood

**sano (adj)**
healthy

**sapo (n) (m)**
toad

**sartén (n) (f)**
frying pan

**seco (adj)**
dry

**sedal (n) (m)**
fishing line

**sediento (adj)**
thirsty

**segundo (adj)**
second

**seguro (adj)**
safe, sure

**sello (n) (m)**
stamp

**selva (n) (f)**
jungle

**selva tropical (n) (f)**
rainforest

**semáforo (n) (f)**
traffic lights

**semana (n) (f)**
week

**semicírculo (n) (m)**
semicircle

**semilla (n) (f)**
seed

**señal (n) (f)**
sign

**sencillo (adj)**
simple

**sentido (n) (m)**
sense

**separado (adv)**
apart

**serpiente (n) (f)**
snake

**servilleta de papel (n) (f)**
paper towel

**siempre (adv)**
always

**significado (n) (m)**
meaning

**silla (n) (f)**
chair

**silla de montar (n) (f)**
saddle (horse)

**silla de ruedas (n) (f)**
wheelchair

**sillín (n) (m)**
saddle (bike)

**sillón (n) (m)**
armchair

**símbolo (n) (m)**
symbol

**simpático (adj)**
friendly

**sin (prep)**
without

**sitio web (n) (m)**
website

**situación (n) (f)**
location

**snowboard (n) (m)**
snowboard

**sobre (n) (m)**
envelope

**sobre (prep)**
about

**sobrino/a (n) (m/f)**
nephew/niece

**socorrista (n) (m)**
lifeguard

**sofá (n) (m)**
sofa

**sol (n) (m)**
sun

**sólamente (adv)**
only

**soleado (adj)**
sunny

**sólido (n) (m)**
solid

**solo (adj)**
alone

**sombra (n) (f)**
shadow

**sombrero (n) (m)**
hat

**sombrilla (n) (f)**
parasol

**sordo (adj)**
deaf

**sorprendente (adj)**
surprising

**sorpresa (n) (f)**
surprise

**sótano (n) (m)**
cellar

**spaghetti (n) (m)**
spaghetti

**su, sus (adj) (sing/plu)**
her, his, its, their

**suave (adj)**
smooth

**submarino (n) (m)**
submarine

**subterráneo (adj)**
underground

**sucio (adj)**
dirty

**sueldo (n) (m)**
pay

**suelo (n) (m)**
floor, ground

**sueño (n) (m)**
dream

**suficiente (adj)**
enough

**superficie (n) (f)**
surface

**supermercado (n) (m)**
supermarket

**sur (n) (m)**
south

**surf (n) (m)**
surfing

**suya, suyo, suyas, suyos (pron)**
hers, his

# T

**tabla (n) (f)**
board

**tabla de surf (n) (f)**
surfboard

**talla (n) (f)**
size

**también (adv)**
also

**tambor (n) (m)**
drum

**tapa (n) (f)**
lid

**tapón (n) (m)**
plug (sink)

**tarde (n) (f)**
afternoon

**tarde (adv)**
late

**tarde noche (n) (f)**
evening

**tarjeta (n) (f)**
card

**tarjeta de cumpleaños (n) (f)**
birthday card

**tarta de cumpleaños (n) (f)**
birthday cake

**taxi (n) (m)**
taxi

**taza (n) (f)**
cup, mug

**té (n) (m)**
tea

**teatro de marionetas (n) (m)**
puppet show

**tebeo (n) (m)**
comic

**techo (n) (m)**
ceiling

**teclado (n) (m)**
keyboard

**tejado (n) (m)**
roof

**tela (n) (f)**
cloth

**teléfono (n) (m)**
phone

**teléfono móvil (n) (m)**
mobile phone

**telescopio (n) (m)**
telescope

**televisión (n) (f)**
television

**tema (n) (m)**
subject

**templado (adj)**
warm (drink)

**temprano (adv)**
early

**tenedor (n) (m)**
fork

**tener éxito (adj)**
popular

**tenis (n) (m)**
tennis

**tenis de mesa (n) (m)**
table tennis

**tercero (adj)**
third

**termómetro (n) (m)**
thermometer

**ternero (n) (m)**
calf

**terrible (adj)**
terrible

**tía (n) (f)**
aunt

**tiburón (n) (m)**
shark

**tiempo (n) (m)**
time (I don't have time), weather

**tiempo libre (n) (m)**
free time

**tienda (n) (f)**
shop, tent

**Tierra (n) (f)**
Earth (planet)

**tierra (n) (f)**
land, soil

**tigre (n) (m)**
tiger

**tijeras (n) (f)**
scissors

**tímido (adj)**
shy

**tinta (n) (f)**
ink

**tío (n) (m)**
uncle

**tipo (adj)**
kind (type)

**toalla (n) (f)**
towel

**toallita (n) (f)**
flannel

**tobillo (n) (m)**
ankle

**todavia (adv)**
still

**todo (adj)**
all

**todo (pron)**
everything

**todo el mundo (pron)**
everybody

**tomate (n) (m)**
tomato

**tormenta de truenos (n) (f)**
thunderstorm

**tormentoso (adj)**
stormy

**tortuga (n) (f)**
tortoise

**tortuga (marina) (n) (f)**
turtle

**tos (n) (f)**
cough

**tostador (n) (m)**
toaster

**trabajo (n) (m)**
job

**tractor (n) (m)**
tractor

**traductor/a (n) (m/f)**
translator

**tráfico (n) (m)**
traffic

**traje (n) (m)**
costume, suit

**tranquilamente (adv)**
quietly

**tranquilo (adj)**
calm, peaceful, quiet

**transporte (n) (m)**
transport

**travieso (adj)**
naughty

**tren (n) (m)**
train

**tren de juguete (n) (m)**
train set

**triangulo (n) (m)**
triangle

**trigo (n) (m)**
wheat

**trimestre (n) (m)**
term

**trineo (n) (m)**
sledge, sleigh

**tripulación (n)**
crew

**triste (adj)**
sad

**trompa (n) (f)**
trunk (animal)

**tronco (n) (m)**
trunk (tree)

**tropical (adj)**
tropical

**trozo (n) (m)**
piece

**tú (pron)**
you

**tu, tus (adj)**
your

**tubo (n) (m)**
tube

**tucán (n) (m)**
toucan

**tumbona (n) (f)**
deck chair

**túnel (n) (m)**
tunnel

**turista (n) (m/f)**
tourist

**turno (n) (m)**
turn

# U

**último (adj)**
last

**un, una (article) (m/f)**
a, an

**uña (n) (f)**
nail

**uniforme (n) (m)**
uniform

**uniforme escolar (n) (m)**
school uniform

**universo (n) (m)**
universe

**unos (article)**
some

**usted, ustedes (pron)**
you

**útil (adj)**
useful

**uva (n) (f)**
grape

# V

**vaca (n) (f)**
cow

**vacaciones (n) (f)**
holiday

**vacío (adj)**
empty

**vago (adj)**
lazy

**valiente (adj)**
brave

**valla (n) (f)**
fence

**vapor (n) (m)**
steam

**vaquero (n) (m)**
cowboy

**vaqueros (n) (m)**
jeans

**varón (adj)**
male

**vaso (n) (m)**
glass (drink)

**vecindario (n) (m)**
neighbourhood

**vecino (n) (m)**
neighbour

**vela (n) (f)**
candle, sail, sailing

**ventana (n) (f)**
window

**ventoso (adj)**
windy

**verano (n) (m)**
summer

**verbo (n) (m)**
verb

**verdadero (adj)**
real, true

**verde (adj)**
green

**verdura (n) (f)**
vegetable

**vestido (n) (m)**
dress

**veterinario/a (n) (m/f)**
vet

**viaje (n) (m)**
journey

**vida (n) (f)**
life

**videojuego (n) (m)**
computer game, video game

**viejo (adj)**
old

**viento (n) (m)**
wind

**violín (n) (m)**
violin

**vosotros (pron)**
you

# Y

**y (conj)**
and

**ya (adv)**
already

**yate (n) (m)**
yacht

**yo (pron)**
I

**yogur (n) (m)**
yoghurt

# Z

**zanahoria (n) (f)**
carrot

**zapatillas (n) (f)**
slippers, trainers

**zapato (n) (m)**
shoe

**zona (n) (f)**
zone

**zoo (n) (m)**
zoo

**zorro (n) (m)**
fox

**zumo (n) (m)**
juice

**zumo de naranja (n) (m)**
orange juice

**zurdo (adj)**
left-handed

# Speaking Spanish

Spanish pronunciation is quite easy. In Spanish you will almost always find that all the letters in a word are pronounced. Once you have learned how to pronounce the letters it is easy to work out how to say a word, even if you have never seen or heard it before.

In this dictionary, we have spelled out each Spanish word in a way that will help you pronounce it. Each syllable should be pronounced as if it were part of an English word.

In our guide, the stress of the word is indicated by capital letters. For example *cuchillo* (knife) = *koo-CHEE-yo – CHEE* is stressed.

Below are a few simple rules to help you with this:

| Our guide | Pronunciation | Example | Our spelling |
|---|---|---|---|
| *th* | is like **th** in "thin" not like **th** in "they". | *cebra* = zebra | *THEH-brah* |
| H | this sound comes from the back of your throat like the Scottish **ch** in "loch". | *gente* = people | *HEN-teh* |
| *s* | with either a single or a double **s** this is like the **s** in "missing", not the **s** in "easy". | *listo* = ready | *LISS-to* |
| *ah* | sounds like "ah", but shorter than in "harm". The sound is not like "hat" but the "ah" is short and sharp. | *más* = more | *mahs* |
| *o* | this is like the **o** in "not" and is even a bit like the **aw** sound in "law". It is not as long as the **o** in "go". | *hola* = hi | *O-lah* |
| *r* | the **r** in Spanish is rolled (on the tip of the tongue) much more than in English, especially at the beginning of a word or syllable. | *perro* = dog | *PAIR-rro* |
| *eh* | the **eh** sound is like the **e** in "met" but slightly longer. | *me* = me | *meh* |

113

# Verbs

This section gives a list of useful verbs (doing words). It shows the infinitive (to ...) of the verb. The most useful verbs, such as "to be" *ser* and *estar* and "to have" *tener*, are written out so that you can see how they change depending on who is doing the action: I = yo; you = tú, usted; he/she = él/ella; we = nosotros/as; you (plural) = vosotros/as, ustedes; ellos/ellas = they.

In Spanish, you use the *usted* and *ustedes* forms of the verb when you want to be polite, especially with someone older than you.

We have written out three of the most regular Spanish verbs: to speak = *hablar*, to eat = *comer* and to live = *vivir*. There is also a reflexive verb written out. Reflexive verbs are often used where you would say "myself" or "yourself" in English. An example is: to wash oneself = *lavarse*.

The verbs that are written out are shown in the present tense – they describe what is happening now or what you normally do.

**to act**
actuar
*ack-too-AR*

**to agree**
estar de acuerdo
*ess-TAR deh ah-koo'ER-do*

**to ask**
preguntar
*preh-goon-TAR*

**to ask for**
pedir
*peh-DEER*

**to bake**
hacer al horno
*ah-THAIR ahl OR-no*

**to bark**
ladrar
*lah-DRAR*

In Spanish there are two verbs for "to be": *ser* and *estar*. *Ser* is used with your name, your profession, your nationality and with descriptions, *estar* with positions and locations and to make the "ing" form of verbs.

**to be**
ser
*sair*
**I am**
yo soy
**you are (singular)**
tú eres
**he, she, (you polite singular) is**
él, ella, (usted) es
**we are**
nosotros/as somos
**you are (plural)**
vosotros/as sois
**they, (you polite plural) are**
ellos, ellas, (ustedes) son

estar
*ess-STAR*
**I am**
yo estoy
**you are (singular)**
tú estás
**he, she, (you polite) is**
él, ella, (usted) está
**we are**
nosotros/as estamos
**you are (plural)**
vosotros/as estáis
**they, (you polite plural) are**
ellos/as, (ustedes) están

**to be able**
poder
*po-DAIR*

**to be born**
nacer
*nah-THAIR*

**to be called**
llamarse
*yah-MAR-seh*

*Hago pasteles al horno.*

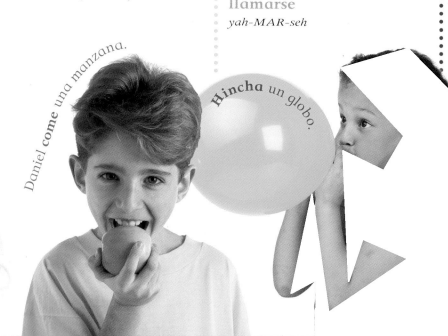

*Daniel come una manzana.*

*Hincha un globo.*

Lucia **lleva** las bolsas.

**to be cold/hot**
tener frío/calor
teh-NAIR FREE-o/kah-LOR

**to be hungry**
tener hambre
teh-NAIR AHM-breh

**to be scared of**
tener miedo de
teh-NAIR mee'EH-do deh

**to be thirsty**
tener sed
teh-NAIR sehd

**to become**
hacerse
ah-THAIR-seh

**to begin**
empezar
em-peh-THAR

**to behave**
comportarse
kom-por-TAR-seh

**to believe**
creer
kree-AIR

**to bend**
doblar
do-BLAR

**to bite**
morder
mor-DAIR

**to blow up (a balloon)**
hinchar (un globo)
in-CHAR

**to borrow**
tomar prestado
to-MAR press-TAH-do

**to bounce**
rebotar
reh-bo-TAR

**to brake**
frenar
freh-NAR

**to break**
romper
rom-PAIR

**to breathe**
respirar
rres-pee-RAR

**to bring**
traer
trah-AIR

**to brush**
cepillar
theh-pee-YAR

**to brush one's teeth**
cepillarse
los dientes
theh-pee-YAR-seh
los dee-EN-tehs

**to build**
construir
kons-troo'EER

**to bump into**
encontrarse
en-kon-TRAR-seh

**to buy**
comprar
kom-PRAR

**to carry**
llevar
yeh-BAR

**to catch**
coger
ko-HAIR

**to cause**
causar
kah'oo-SAR

**to celebrate**
celebrar
theh-leh-BRAR

**to change**
cambiar
kahm-be-AR

**to charge (a phone)**
cargar
kar-GAR

**to check**
comprobar
kom-pro-BAR

**to choose**
elegir
eh-leh-HEER

**to clean**
limpiar
lim-pee-AR

**to clear**
despejar
dess-peh-HAR

**Coge** la pelota.

115

**to climb**
escalar
*ess-kah-LAR*

**to close**
cerrar
*theh-RRAR*

**to collect**
recolectar
*rreh-ko-lek-TAR*

**to come**
venir
*beh-NEER*

**to come back**
volver
*bol-BAIR*

**to come from**
venir de
*beh-NEER deh*

**to compare**
comparar
*kom-pah-RAR*

**to complain**
quejarse
*keh-HAR-seh*

**to contain**
contener
*kon-teh-NAIR*

**to continue**
continuar
*kon-tee-noo-AR*

**to cook**
cocinar
*ko-thi-NAR*

**to copy**
copiar
*ko-pee-AR*

**to cost**
costar
*kos-TAR*

**to count**
contar
*kon-TAR*

**to cover**
cubrir
*koo-BREER*

**to crack**
abrir
*ah-BREER*

**to crash**
chocar
*cho-KAR*

**to create**
crear
*kreh-AR*

**to cross**
cruzar
*kroo-THAR*

**to cry**
llorar
*yo-RAR*

**to cut**
cortar
*kor-TAR*

**to cut out**
recortar
*reh-kor-TAR*

**to cycle**
montar en bicicleta
*mon-TAR en be-thi-KLEH-tah*

**to dance**
bailar
*bah'e-LAR*

**to decide**
decidir
*deh-thi-DEER*

**to decorate**
decorar
*deh-ko-RAR/ah-dor-NAR*

**to describe**
describir
*dess-kree-beer*

**to die**
morir
*mo-REER*

**to dig**
excavar
*eks-kah-BAR*

Cristina **baila** bien.

Ana **cava** en la arena.

Alberto **hace** el jardín.

**to disappear**

desaparecer
dess-ah-pah-reh-THAIR

**to discover**

descubrir
dess-koo-BREER

**to dive**

tirase de cabeza
tee-RAH-seh deh kah-BEH-thah

**to do**

hacer
ah-THAIR

I do
yo hago
you do
tú haces
he, she, (you polite) does
él, ella, (usted) hace
we do
nosotros/as hacemos
you do (plural)
vosotros/as hacéis
they, (you polite plural) do
ellos/as, (ustedes) hacen

**to do the gardening**

hacer el jardín
ah-THAIR ell Har-DEEN

**to draw**

dibujar
dee-boo-HAR

**to dream**

soñar
so-N'YAR

**to dress up**

disfrazarse
diss-frah-THAR-seh

**to drink**

beber
beh-BAIR

**to drive**

conducir
kon-doo-THEER

**to dry**

secar
seh-KAR

**to earn**

ganar
gah-NAR

**to eat**

comer
ko-MAIR

I eat
yo como
you eat
tú comes
he, she, (you polite) eats
él, ella, (usted) come
we eat
nosotros/as comemos
you eat (plural)
vosotros/as coméis
they, (you polite plural) eat
ellos/as, (ustedes) comen

**to encourage**

animar
ah-nee-MAR

Estoy comiendo pastel de chocolate.

**to enjoy**

disfrutar
diss-froo-TAR

**to escape**

escapar
ess-kah-PAR

**to explain**

explicar
eks-plee-KAR

**to fall**

caer
kah-AIR

**to fall down**

caerse
kah-AIR-seh

**to feed**

dar de comer
dar deh ko-MAIR

**to feel**

sentir
sen-TEER

**to fetch**

traer
trah-AIR

**to fight**

pelear
peh-leh-AR

**to fill**

llenar
yeh-NAR

¡Da de comer a los perros!

117

**to find**
encontrar
*en-kon-TRAR*

**to find out**
averiguar
*ah-beh-ree-goo'AR*

**to finish**
terminar
*ter-min-AR*

**to fit**
caber
*kah-BAIR*

**to float**
flotar
*flo-TAR*

**to fly**
volar
*bo-LAR*

**to fold**
doblar
*do-BLAR*

**to follow**
seguir
*seh-GHEER*

**to forget**
olvidar
*ol-be-DAR*

**to freeze**
congelar
*kon-Heh-LAR*

**to frighten**
asustar
*ah-soos-TAR*

**to get**
obtener
*ob-teh-NAIR*

*Dobla* el papel.

**to get on (a bus)**
subirse
*suh-BEER-seh*

**to get ready**
prepararse
*preh-pah-RAR-seh*

**to get up**
levantarse
*lev-an-TAR-seh*

**to give**
dar
*dar*

**to go**
ir
*eer*

**I go**
yo voy
**you go**
tú vas
**he, she, (you polite) go**
él, ella, (usted) va
**we go**
nosotros/as vamos
**you go (plural)**
vosotros/as váis
**they, (you polite plural) go**
ellos/as, (ustedes) van

**to go camping**
ir de camping
*eer deh KAM-ping*

**to go on holiday**
ir de vacaciones
*eer deh bah-kah-thi-O-nes*

**to go out**
salir
*sah-LEER*

**to go shopping**
ir de compras
*eer deh KOM-prahs*

**to grow**
crecer
*kreh-THAIR*

**to guess**
adivinar
*ah-dee-be-NAR*

**to hang up (phone)**
colgar
*kol-GAR*

**to happen**
suceder
*soo-theh-DAIR*

**to hate**
odiar
*o-dee-AR*

**to have**
tener
*teh-NAIR*

**I have**
yo tengo
**you have**
tú tienes
**he, she, (you polite) has**
él, ella, (usted) tiene
**we have**
nosotros/as tenemos
**you have (plural)**
vosotros/as tenéis
**they, (you polite plural) have**
ellos/as, (ustedes) tienen

*Carlos desayuna tostades y huevos.*

*María se está divirtiendo.*

**to jump**
saltar
*sahl-TAR*

**to keep**
mantener
*mahn-teh-NAIR*

**to keep warm**
abrigar
*ah-bree-GAR*

**to kick**
dar una patada
*dar OO-nah pah-TAH-dah*

**to kill**
matar
*mah-TAR*

**to have a bath**
bañarse
*bah-N'YAH-seh*

**to have a shower**
ducharse
*doo-CHAR-seh*

**to have breakfast**
desayunar
*dess-ah-yoo-NAR*

**to have dinner**
cenar
*theh-NAR*

**to have fun**
divertirse
*dee-bair-TEER-seh*

**to hear**
oír
*o'EER*

**to help**
ayudar
*ah-yoo-DAR*

**to hide**
esconder
*ess-kon-DAIR*

**to hit**
pegar
*peh-GAR*

**to hold**
sujetar
*soo-He-TAR*

**to hop**
dar saltos
*dar SAHL-tos*

**to hope**
esperar
*ess-peh-RAR*

**to hurry**
darse prisa
*DAR-seh PREE-sah*

**to hurt (oneself)**
hacerse daño
*ah-THAIR-seh DAH-n'yo*

**to imagine**
imaginar
*ee-mah-He-NAR*

**to include**
incluir
*in-kloo-EER*

**to inspire**
inspirar
*ins-pee-RAR*

**to invent**
inventar
*in-ben-TAR*

**to invite**
invitar
*in-be-TAR*

**to join**
unirse
*oo-NEER-seh*

**to kiss**
besar
*beh-SAR*

**to know**
saber
*sah-BAIR*

**to land (in a plane)**
aterrizar
*ah-ter-rree-THAR*

**to last**
durar
*doo-RAR*

**to laugh**
reírse
*reh-EER-seh*

**to lay a table**
poner la mesa
*po-NAIR lah MEH-sah*

**to lead**
dirigir
*dee-ree-HEER*

*Las ranas dan grandes saltos por el aire.*

119

**to learn**
aprender
ah-pren-DAIR

**to lie**
mentir
men-TEER

**to lift**
levantar
leh-bahn-TAR

**to like**
gustar
goos-TAR

**to listen (to)**
escuchar
ess-koo-CHAR

**to live**
vivir
be-BEER
I live
yo vivo
**you live**
tú vives
**he, she, (you polite) lives**
él, ella, (usted) vive
**we live**
nosotros/as vivimos
**you live (plural)**
vosotros/as vivis
**they, (you polite plural) live**
ellos/as, (ustedes) viven

**to lock**
cerrar con llave
thair-RAR kon YAH-beh

Juan **escucha** música.

**to look**
mirar
mee-RAR

**to look after**
cuidar
koo'ee-DAR

**to look for**
buscar
boos-KAR

**to lose**
perder
pair-DAIR

**to love**
querer
keh-RAIR

**to make**
hacer
ah-THAIR

**to make a wish**
pedir un deseo
peh-DEER oon deh-SEH-o

**to make friends**
hacer amigos
ah-THAIR ah-MEE-gos

**to marry**
casarse
kah-SAR-seh

**to mean**
querer decir
keh-RAIR deh-THEER

**to measure**
medir
meh-DEER

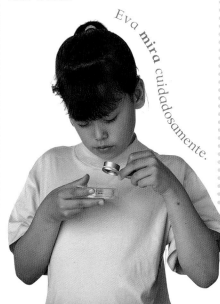

Eva **mira** cuidadosamente.

Rosa **abre** la puerta.

**to meet**
quedar con
keh-DAR kon

**to mix**
mezclar
meth-KLAR

**to move**
mover
mo-BAIR

**to need**
necesitar
neh-theh-see-TAR

**to not feel well**
encontrarse mal
en-kon-TRAR-seh mahl

**to notice**
notar
no-TAR

**to offer**
ofrecer
o-freh-THAIR

**to open**
abrir
ah-BREER

**to own**
tener
teh-NAIR

**to pack**
hacer la maleta
ah-THAIR lah mah-LEH-tah

**to paint**
pintar
pin-TAR

**to pay**
pagar
*pah-GAR*

**to persuade**
persuadir
*pair-soo'ah-DEER*

**to pick up**
recoger
*rreh-ko-HAIR*

**to plan**
planear
*plahn-TAR*

**to plant**
plantar
*plah-neh-AR*

**to play**
jugar
*Hoo-GAR*

**to play an instrument**
tocar un instrumento
*to-KAR oon in-stroo-MEN-to*

**to point**
apuntar
*ah-poon-TAR*

**to pour**
echar
*eh-CHAR*

**to practise**
practicar
*prak-tee-KAR*

**to predict**
predecir
*preh-deh-THEER*

**to prefer**
preferir
*preh-feh-REER*

**to prepare**
preparar
*preh-pah-RAR*

**to press**
prensar
*pren-SAR*

**to pretend**
pretender
*preh-ten-DAIR*

**to print**
imprimir
*im-pree-MEER*

**to produce**
producir
*pro-doo-THEER*

**to programme**
programar
*pro-grah-MAR*

**to promise**
prometer
*pro-meh-TER*

**to protect**
proteger
*pro-teh-HAIR*

**to provide**
proporcionar
*pro-por-thi-o-NAR*

**to pull**
tirar
*tee-RAR*

**to push**
empujar
*em-poo-HAR*

**to put**
poner
*po-NAIR*

**to put away**
guardar
*goo'ar-DAR*

**to rain**
llover
*yo-BAIR*

**to reach**
alcanzar
*ahl-kahn-THAR*

**to read**
leer
*leh-AIR*

¿Puedes **pintar** un cuadro?

¡**Echa** el agua con cuidado!

**to realise**
darse cuenta
*DAR-seh koo'EN-tah*

**to recognise**
reconocer
*rreh-ko-no-THAIR*

**to refuse**
rechazar
*rreh-chah-THAR*

**to relax**
relajarse
*rreh-lah-HAR-seh*

**to remain**
quedar
*keh-DAR*

**to remember**
recordar
*rreh-kor-DAR*

**to repair**
reparar
*rreh-pah-RAR*

**to rest**
descansar
*dess-kahn-SAR*

**to return**
regresar
*rreh-greh-SAR*

**to ride a bike**
montar en bicicleta
*mon-TAR en be-thi-KLEH-tah*

**to ride a horse**
montar a caballo
*mon-TAR ah kah-BAH-yo*

Pablo **corre** rápido.

**to ring**
llamar
*yah-MAR*

**to roll**
enrollar
*en-ro-YAR*

**to rub**
frotar
*fro-TAR*

**to run**
correr
*kor-RRER*

**to run after**
perseguir
*pair-seh-goo'EER*

**to save**
ahorrar
*ah-o-RRAR*

**to say**
decir
*deh-THEER*

**to score (a goal)**
marcar
*mar-KAR*

**to scratch**
rascar
*rahs-KAR*

**to search**
buscar
*boos-KAR*

**to see**
ver
*bair*

**to seem**
parecer
*pah-reh-THAIR*

Raquel **lee** su libro.

**to sell**
vender
*ven-DAIR*

**to send**
enviar
*en-be-AR*

**to share**
compartir
*kom-par-TEER*

**to shine**
brillar
*bree-YAR*

**to shout**
gritar
*gree-TAR*

**to show**
mostrar
*moss-TRAR*

**to sing**
cantar
*kahn-TAR*

**to sit**
estar sentado/a
*ess-TAR sen-TAH-do/ah*

Mónica **monta** su caballo.

**to sit down**
sentarse
*sen-TAR-seh*

**to skate**
patinar
*pah-tee-NAR*

**to ski**
esquiar
*ess-kee-AR*

**to sleep**
dormir
*dor-MEER*

**to slide**
deslizarse
*dess-lee-THAR-seh*

**to slip**
resbalar
*rres-bah-LAR*

**to smell**
oler
*o-LAIR*

**to smile**
sonreír
*son-reh-EER*

**to snow**
nevar
*neh-BAR*

**to sound (like)**
sonar (como)
*so-NAR*

*Ángel está durmiendo.*

**to speak**
hablar
*ah-BLAR*

**I speak**
yo hablo
**you speak**
tú hablas
**he, she, (you polite) speaks**
él, ella, (usted) habla
**we speak**
nosotros/as hablamos
**you speak (plural)**
vosotros/as habláis
**they (you polite plural) speak**
ellos/as, (ustedes) hablan

**to spell**
deletrear
*deh-leh-treh-AR*

**to spin**
dar vueltas
*dar boo'EL-tahs*

**to spread**
extender
*eks-ten-DAIR*

**to stand**
estar de pie
*ess-TAR deh pee'EH*

**to stand up**
ponerse de pie
*po-NAIR-seh deh pee'EH*

**to start**
empezar
*em-peh-THAR*

**to stay**
quedarse
*keh-DAR-seh*

*Lucía le **grita** a su amigo.*

**to steer**
conducir
*kon-doo-THEER*

**to stick**
pegar
*peh-GAR*

**to sting**
picar
*pee-KAR*

**to stop**
parar
*pah-RAR*

**to stretch**
estirar
*ess-tee-RAR*

**to study**
estudiar
*ess-too-dee-AR*

**to surf**
hacer surf
*ah-THAIR soorf*

**to surprise**
sorprender
*sor-pren-DAIR*

**to survive**
sobrevivir
*so-breh-be-BEER*

**to swim**
nadar
*nah-DAR*

*Extender el chocolate en los pasteles.*

123

*La niña saca una foto.*

**to take**
tomar
*to-MAR*

**to take a photo**
sacar una foto
*sah-KAR oona FO-toh*

**to take away**
quitar
*kee-TAR*

**to take turns**
hacer turnos
*ah-THAIR TOOR-nos*

**to talk**
hablar
*ah-BLAR*

**to tap**
dar golpecitos
*dar gol-peh-THEE-tos*

**to tape**
grabar
*grah-BAR*

**to taste**
probar
*pro-BAR*

**to teach**
enseñar
*en-seh-N'YAR*

**to tease**
tomar el pelo
*to-MAR ell PEH-lo*

**to tell**
contar
*kon-TAR*

**to tell a story**
contar una historia
*kon-TAR oo-nah iss-TOH-ree-ah*

**to tell the time**
decir la hora
*deh-THEER lah O-rah*

**to thank**
agradecer
*ah-grah-deh-THAIR*

**to think**
pensar
*pen-SAR*

**to throw**
tirar
*tee-RAR*

**to tidy up**
recoger
*rreh-ko-HAIR*

**to tie**
atar
*ah-TAR*

**to touch**
tocar
*to-KAR*

**to train**
entrenar
*en-treh-NAR*

**to translate**
traducir
*trah-doo-THEER*

**to travel**
viajar
*be-ah-HAR*

*Isabel está pensando.*

**to treat (well)**
tratar (bien)
*trah-TAR (be-EN)*

**to try**
intentar
*in-ten-TAR*

**to try on**
probar
*pro-BAR*

**to turn**
girar
*Hee-RAR*

**to twist**
enrollar
*en-ro-YAR*

**to type**
escribir (a máquina)
*ess-kree-BEER (ah MAH-kee-nah)*

**to understand**
entender
*en-ten-DAIR*

**to undo**
deshacer
*dess-ah-THAIR*

**to undress**
desnudarse
*dess-noo-DAR-seh*

**to unpack**
deshacer la maleta
*dess-ah-THAIR lah mah-LEH-tah*

*¡Tira el balón, Luis!*

**to use**
usar
*oo-SAR*

**to visit**
visitar
*be-see-TAR*

**to wait**
esperar
*ess-peh-RAR*

**to wake up**
despertarse
*dess-pair-TAR-seh*

**to walk**
andar
*ahn-DAR*

**to want**
querer
*keh-RAIR*

**I want**
yo quiero
**you want**
tú quieres
**he, she, (you polite) wants**
él, ellas, (usted) quiere
**we want**
nosotros/as queremos
**you want (plural)**
vosotros/as queréis
**they, (you polite plural) want**
ellos, ellas, (ustedes) quieren

Jaime **escribe** un correo electrónico.

Laura **lava los platos**.

**to warm**
calentarse
*kah-len-TAR-seh*

**to wash**
lavar
*lah-BAR*

**to wash (oneself)**
lavarse
*lah-BAH-seh*

**I wash myself**
yo me lavo
**you wash yourself**
tú te lavas
**he, she, (you polite) washes himself**
él, ellas, (usted) se lava
**we wash ourselves**
nosotros/as nos lavamos
**you wash yourselves**
vosotros/as os laváis
**they, (you polite plural) wash themselves**
ellos/as, (ustedes) se lavan

**to wash the dishes**
fregar los platos
*freh-GAR los PLAH-tos*

**to watch**
ver
*bair*

**to wave**
saludar
*sah-loo-DAR*

**to wear**
llevar (puesto)
*ye-BAR (poo'ESS-to)*

**to weigh**
pesar
*peh-SAR*

**to whisper**
susurrar
*soo-soor-RRAR*

**to win**
ganar
*gah-NAR*

**to wish**
desear
*deh-seh-AR*

**to wonder**
preguntarse
*preh-goon-TAR-seh*

**to work**
trabajar
*trah-bah-HAR*

**to work (function)**
funcionar
*foon-thi-o-NAR*

**to wrap**
envolver
*en-bol-BAIR*

**to write**
escribir
*ess-kree-BEER*

Eduardo **escribe** en su diario.

125

# Useful phrases

## *Frases de utilidad*

**Learn the days of the week**

**Monday**
lunes
*LOO-ness*

**Tuesday**
martes
*MAR-tess*

**Wednesday**
miércoles
*mee-AIR-ko-less*

**Thursday**
jueves
*Hoo'EH-bess*

**Friday**
viernes
*be-AIR-ness*

**Saturday**
sabado
*SAH-bah-do*

**Sunday**
domingo
*do-MEEN-go*

**Yes**
Sí
*see*

**No**
No
*no*

**Hello**
Hola
*O-lah*

**Goodbye**
Adiós
*ah-dee-OS*

**See you later**
Hasta luego
*AHS-tah loo-EH-go*

**Please**
Por favor
*por fah-BOR*

**Thank you**
Gracias
*GRAH-thi-ahs*

**Excuse me**
Perdón
*pair-DON*

**I'm sorry**
Lo siento
*lo see-EN-to*

**My name is...**
Me llamo...
*meh YAH-mo*

**I live in...**
Vivo en...
*BE-bo en*

**I am...years old.**
Tengo...años
*TEN-go...AH-n'yos*

**I don't understand**
No entiendo
*no en-tee-EN-do*

**I don't know**
No sé
*no seh*

**Very well**
Muy bien
*moo'e be-EN*

**Very much**
Mucho
*MOO-cho*

**I do/don't like...**
Me gusta/no me gusta
*meh GOOS-tah/no meh GOOS-tah*

**Let's go!**
¡Vamos!
*BAH-mos*

**Happy Birthday!**
¡Feliz cumpleaños!
*feh-LEETH koom-pleh-AH-n'yos*

*Hola, me llamo Luca.*

**How are you?**
¿Cómo estás?
*KO-mo ess-TAHS*

**What is your name?**
¿Cómo te llamas?
*KO-mo teh YAH-mahs*

**Do you speak…?**
¿Hablas…?
*AH-blahs*

**Do you like…?**
¿Te gusta…?
*teh GOOS-tah*

**Do you have…?**
¿Tienes…?
*tee-EH-ness*

**Can I have…?**
¿Puedes darme…?
*poo-EH-dess DAR-meh*

**How much…?**
¿Cuánto cuesta…?
*koo'AHN-to koo'ESS-tah*

**How many?**
¿Cuántos/as?
*koo'AHN-toss/ahs*

**Can you help me?**
¿Puedes ayudarme?
*poo-EH-dess ah-yoo-DAR-meh*

**What time is it?**
¿Qué hora es?
*keh O-rah ess*

**What's that?**
¿Qué es eso?
*keh ess ESS-o*

**Help!**
¡Socorro!
*so-KOR-rro*

**Stop!**
¡Para!
*PAH-rah*

**Turn right/left**
Gira a la derecha/izquierda
*HE-rah a lah deh-REH-cha/*
*ith-kee'AIR-dah*

**Go straight on**
Sigue todo recto
*SEE-geh TO-do RREK-to*

**In front of**
Delante de
*deh-LAHN-teh deh*

**Next to**
Al lado de
*ahl LAH-do deh*

**Where is/are…?**
¿Dónde está/n…?
*DON-deh ess-TAH/TAHN*

*Learn the months of the year*

**January**
enero
*eh-NAIR-ro*

**February**
febrero
*feh-BRAIR-ro*

**March**
marzo
*MAR-tho*

**April**
abril
*ah-BREEL*

**May**
mayo
*MAH-yo*

**June**
junio
*HOO-nee-o*

**July**
julio
*HOO-lee-o*

**August**
agosto
*ah-GOS-to*

**September**
septiembre
*sep-tee-EM-breh*

**October**
octubre
*ok-TOO-breh*

**November**
noviembre
*no-be-EM-breh*

**December**
diciembre
*dee-thi-EM-breh*

¡Vámonos!

*Useful phraes*

# Los números

## *Numbers*

**0 cero**
*THEH-ro*
zero

**1 uno**
*OO-no*
one

**2 dos**
*doss*
two

**3 tres**
*trehs*
three

**4 cuatro**
*koo-AH-tro*
four

**5 cinco**
*THEEN-ko*
five

**6 seis**
*SEH-iss*
six

**7 siete**
*see-EH-teh*
seven

**8 ocho**
*O-cho*
eight

**9 nueve**
*noo'EH-beh*
nine

**10 diez**
*dee-ETH*
ten

**11 once**
*ON-theh*
eleven

**12 doce**
*DO-theh*
twelve

**13 trece**
*TREH-theh*
thirteen

**14 catorce**
*kah-TOR-theh*
fourteen

**15 quince**
*KEEN-theh*
fifteen

**16 dieciséis**
*dee-eh-thi-SEH-iss*
sixteen

**17 diecisiete**
*dee-eh-thi-see-EH-teh*
seventeen

**18 dieciocho**
*dee-eh-thi-O-cho*
eighteen

**19 diecinueve**
*dee-eh-thi-noo'EH-beh*
nineteen

**20 veinte**
*BE-in-teh*
twenty

**21 veintiuno**
*be-in-tee-OO-no*
twenty-one

**30 treinta**
*treh-IN-tah*
thirty

**40 cuarenta**
*koo'ar-EN-tah*
fourty

**50 cincuenta**
*thin-koo'EN-tah*
fifty

**60 sesenta**
*seh-SEN-tah*
sixty

**70 setenta**
*seh-TEN-tah*
seventy

**80 ochenta**
*o-CHEN-tah*
eighty

**90 noventa**
*no-BEN-tah*
ninety

**100 cien**
*thi-EN*
one hundred

## Acknowledgements

DK would like to thank the following people: Sarah Ponder and Carole Oliver for design help; Jennie Morris, Lucy Heaver and Marie Greenwood for editorial help; Angela Wilkes for language consultancy; Katherine Northam for digital artwork; Rose Horridge for picture research; Rachael Swann for picture research assistance; and Hope Annets, Mary Mead, Bethany Tombs, Todd and Sophie Yonwin for modelling. The publisher would like to thank the following for their kind permission to reproduce their photographs: (Key: t = top, b = bottom, r = right, l = left, c = centre) 31: www.aviationpictures.com/Austin J. Brown 1983 (tl); 31: Courtesy of FSTOP Pte. Ltd., Singapore (tc); 54: Corbis/Ronnie Kaufman (br); 55: Corbis/Craig Tuttle (tl); 55: Corbis/Craig Tuttle (tr); 55: Zefa/J. Jaemsen (cl); 55: Zefa/J. Jaemsen (cr); 55: Powerstock (bl); 72: Getty Images/Stone/Stuart Westmorland (tl); 82: Indianapolis Motor Speedway Foundation, Inc. (tc); 91: David Edge (tc); 91: Courtesy of Junior Department, Royal College of Music, London (br). All other images © Dorling Kindersley. For further information see www.dkimages.com

Los números